10

MINUTE GUIDE TO

pcANYWHERE™

by Sue Plumley

A Division of Macmillan Computer Publishing
201 W. 103rd St., Indianapolis, IN 46290 USA

Dedicated to my friend and fellow author, Elaine Marmel, for being supportive, understanding, contributive, and sympathetic.

©1997 by Que® Corporation

Library of Congress Catalog Card Number: 12695-7

International Standard Book Number: 0-7897-1269-5

98 97 96   8 7 6 5 4 3 2 1

Interpretation of the printing code: the rightmost double-digit number is the year of the book's first printing; the rightmost single-digit number is the number of the book's printing. For example, a printing code of 96-1 shows that this copy of the book was printed during the first printing of the book in 1996.

Printed in the United States of America

Publisher Roland Elgey

Vice President and Publisher Joe Wilkert

Publishing Manager Karen Reinisch

Editorial Services Director Elizabeth Keaffaber

Managing Editor Thomas F. Hayes

Acquisitions Editor Martha O'Sullivan

Technical Specialist Nadeem Muhammed

Product Development Specialist Melanie Palaisa

Production Editor Kathryn Purdum

Acqustions Coordinator Michelle Newcomb

Book Designer Barbara Kordesh

Cover Designer Dan Armstrong

Production Team Bryan Flores, Jessica Ford, Christy Hendershot, Anjy Perry, Nicole Ruessler

Indexer Tim Wright

Special thanks to Christina Gleeson for ensuring the technical accuracy of this book.

CONTENTS

Introduction

pcANYWHERE offers communications solutions for your network or standalone computer. You can use the program in a variety of ways to remotely control other computers, attach to a network as a node, and transfer files between computers. pcANYWHERE is a powerful program you can use for all of your communications needs.

Why pcANYWHERE?

pcANYWHERE offers remote control, file transfer, and general communications solutions to your network or standalone computer. Specifically, pcANYWHERE enables you to remotely control one PC from another. For example, you can use pcANYWHERE to access your work computer from home, performing all the keystrokes and file tasks you would if you were actually sitting at your desk. pcANYWHERE puts the host computer's entire desktop right on the remote controlling desktop, while still giving the remote control PC access to its own desktop, files, and applications.

Additionally, pcANYWHERE enables you to transfer files and folders between two PCs. You can send files (upload) to someone else's PC as well as receive files (download) from another PC, with the click of a mouse, a modem, and a phone line.

Finally, pcANYWHERE enables you to connect to your company's network by cable or phone line and take advantage of files, folders, printers, and other resources offered by the network. Connecting through pcANYWHERE makes your computer a network node like any workstation that is actually attached to the network.

You can use pcANYWHERE in the following ways:

- Call an online service such as a bulletin board or information service to transfer files, e-mail, research libraries, and so on.

- Establish your computer as a host to be accessed by other remote users, for transferring files, or accessing other resources.

- Remotely control a host computer for the purpose of troubleshooting problems, accessing data and resources, and so on.

- Transfer files to and from a host computer.

- Act as a gateway that enables users to share a modem.

- Attach to a network remotely to take advantage of resources and files.

Additionally, pcANYWHERE runs on both Windows 95 and Windows NT 3.51 or 4.0 (Workstation and Server); however, pcANYWHERE parallel connections do not support Windows NT 3.51. You can connect computers using pcANYWHERE with telephone lines and a modem, a network connection, or a combination of both. Additionally, you can directly cable two computers using either a serial or parallel cable and use pcANYWHERE to share data and files between the two.

WHY THE 10 MINUTE GUIDE TO pcANYWHERE?

The *10 Minute Guide to pcANYWHERE* can save you time and effort when learning the software. Each lesson is designed so that you can complete it in 10 minutes or less, so you'll be up-to-snuff in using pcANYWHERE quickly.

Although you can jump between lessons, starting at the beginning is a good plan. The bare-bones basics are covered first, and the more advanced topics are covered later. Also, if you need help installing the software, check out Appendix A for installation instructions on the various uses of the program, hardware requirements, and first time configuration of pcANYWHERE.

CONVENTIONS USED IN THIS BOOK

To help you move through the lessons easily, I've used the following conventions:

On-screen text   On-screen text appears in bold type.

What you type   Information you type appears in bold color type.

Options and commands   Commands, options, and icons you select as well as keys you press appear in color type.

In telling you to choose menu commands, this book uses the format *menu name, menu command*. For example, if the book reads, say "choose File, Properties," you are to open the File Menu and select the Properties command.

In addition to these conventions, the *10 Minute Guide to pcANYWHERE* uses the following icons to identify helpful information:

Plain English tips define new terms or terms that may be unfamiliar to you, such as technical terminology, jargon, and so on.

Timesaver Tip icons show different keyboard and mouse shortcuts and hints that can save you time and energy.

Panic Button icons identify areas where new users often run into trouble, and offer practical solutions to those problems.

TRADEMARKS

All terms mentioned in this book that are known to be trade-marks have been appropriately capitalized. Que cannot attest to the accuracy of this information. Use of a term in this book should not be regarded as affecting the validity of any trademark or service mark.

GETTING STARTED WITH pcANYWHERE

In this lesson, you learn how to start and exit pcANYWHERE, to use the screen, and to understand pcANYWHERE.

UNDERSTANDING pcANYWHERE

pcANYWHERE is a program you can use to connect to remote computers for various reasons. You might want to call your office computer from home, for example, to work from home. You can attach to that computer over the phone lines, and using pcANY-WHERE, you can work as if you were sitting at your desk at the office.

Another task you can perform with pcANYWHERE is file transfer. You can connect to another computer, and then upload and download files. Send and receive word processing files (correspondence, reports, memos), spreadsheets (quarterly reports, finance sheets, charts), databases (customer files, address lists, product information), and so on.

 Upload/Download   When you upload files, you transfer copies of files from your local computer to a distant computer using a modem or the network. Downloading files means to transfer a copy of the files from a distant computer to your local computer over a modem or network.

You also can use pcANYWHERE to connect to a network as a *workstation*, or *node*. Suppose your company has a network to which you are attached when at the office. However, when you're on the road you use a laptop. You can use pcANYWHERE to dial up the office and attach to the network, taking advantage of files, folders, printers, and other network resources.

If you're a consultant or you provide technical support to your customers, you can use pcANYWHERE to connect to a customer's PC from your office or on the road, and monitor the user's actions or remotely control the user's actions.

pcANYWHERE has many applications and many benefits. You'll learn more about the program as you work through this book.

You can use pcANYWHERE on the following:

- **Network server**   Install pcANYWHERE to a network server, such as Novell NetWare or NT Server. Workstations can then install the program quickly from the network and use shared folders on the server to store files, get pcANYWHERE help, and so on.

- **Network workstation**   Install pcANYWHERE to a workstation and use the program for file transfers, remote control, online services, and so on. When installed to a workstation, pcANYWHERE can be used over the network or with a modem, if a modem is installed to the workstation or made available through the network.

 Is the Server Down?   If you installed pcANYWHERE to your workstation from the server, the server must be running and you must be attached to access pcANYWHERE.

- **Standalone computer**   pcANYWHERE installed to a standalone computer can make use of all of the program's benefits by way of a modem or by attaching directly to another computer by cable, as long as the other computer also has pcANYWHERE installed. If you use a cable to attach two computers together, the two computers must be in close proximity.

STARTING AND EXITING
pcANYWHERE

You start the pcANYWHERE application from the Start menu, as you would most Windows applications. If you need help installing pcANYWHERE, see Appendix A for more information.

To start pcANYWHERE, follow these steps:

1. Choose Start, Programs, and the pcANYWHERE32 folder. If you installed the program to a different folder than the default, open that folder instead.

2. Choose pcANYWHERE from the menu. The program opens in a restored window on the desktop.

 TIP　**Enlarge the Window**　You can enlarge the window, if you want, by clicking the Maximize button in the title bar of the program.

To exit pcANYWHERE, do one of the following:

- Choose File, Exit.
- Click the Control menu button and choose Close.
- Click the Close (X) button in the title bar.
- Press Alt+F4.
- Click the Exit button on the Action bar.

USING THE **pcANYWHERE** SCREEN

The pcANYWHERE screen consists of menus and tools you can use to perform the tasks you need to connect. Figure 1.1 shows the pcANYWHERE screen, maximized to fill the desktop. Table 1.1 explains the screen elements.

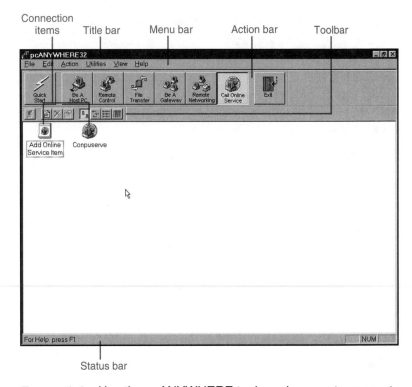

FIGURE 1.1   Use the pcANYWHERE tools and menus to connect to various computers and services.

Connection Item   A connection is a communications link between two computers; a connection item is an icon (small picture) and name that represents the files containing the configuration necessary for the connection. An item may contain, for example, the name and configuration of the modem, the port used, phone number of the service, and any specific commands needed to connect to the service.

TABLE 1.1   pcANYWHERE SCREEN ELEMENTS

ELEMENT	DESCRIPTION
Title bar	Contains the Control menu button, name of the program, and the Minimize, Maximize (or Restore), and Close buttons.
Menu bar	Consist of menus you can choose to perform various commands in the program.
Action bar	Includes buttons that display related services; for example, click the Call Online Service button to view any services you've configured as well as a tool to create online service connections.
Toolbar	Contains tool buttons that provide shortcuts to certain procedures, such as changing the view or adding a new connection. The toolbar displays only when you first select a service from the Action bar.
Status bar	Includes information to help you work in pcANYWHERE, such as descriptions of commands you select and information about connection time.

TIP Show the Action bar, status bar, or toolbar. If you do not see the Action bar, status bar, or toolbar on-screen, choose View and then select the item you want to view. A check mark beside the item means the item is displayed. You cannot view the toolbar unless you first choose a service from the Action bar.

CHANGING VIEWS IN pcANYWHERE

The pcANYWHERE window displays the types of connections you have created (see Appendix B for more information). You can change the way you view these connections, if you want. By default, pcANYWHERE displays the connection items in large icon form. You can also change the view to the following:

- **Large icon view**   Displays the connection items as icons with names below them.

- **Small icon view**   Displays the items with a small icon and the name beside the icon; small icon view displays items from left to right and then from top to bottom.

- **List**   Displays small icons and the name of each item. List view shows the items from top to bottom in a list format.

- **Detail view**   Displays each item with a small icon and its name; also displayed is the phone number, emulation, protocol, and any other pertinent information related to the item.

Before changing the view, you must choose an action (service) from the Action bar. To change views, use the View menu or the View tool buttons on the toolbar. Choose View, and then Large Icons, Small Icons, List, or Detail.

In this lesson, you learned about starting and exiting pcANY-WHERE, using the pcANYWHERE screen, and changing views in the program. In the next lesson, you learn about getting help in pcANYWHERE.

GETTING HELP

In this lesson, you learn how to use the program's Help feature.

USING THE INTRODUCING pcANYWHERE HELP

Whether you're new to pcANYWHERE or only new to version 7.5, you can get help to answer your questions quickly, without wading through terms, definitions, and pages of online help.

To get answers to your immediate questions, follow these steps:

1. Choose Help, Introducing pcANYWHERE.

2. The pcANYWHERE Help screen appears, as shown in Figure 2.1.

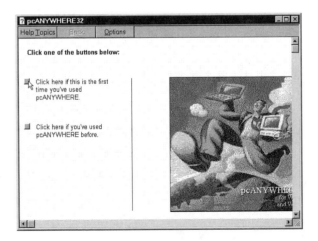

FIGURE 2.1 Get answers to specific questions in this Help screen.

3. Choose one of the following options:

- Choose the First Time You've Used pcANYWHERE option if you want answers to very basic questions, such as What is remote computing? How can I transfer files? How can I get started? and so on.

- Choose the If You've Used pcANYWHERE Before option to find answers to questions about upgraded features.

4. When you choose the option you want to view, Help displays the questions on-screen. Click the question to view the answers. The Help window is divided into two panes: The left pane contains more questions and the right pane contains answers.

5. Continue to scroll the answers or select new questions.

6. To return to the previous Help screen, click the Back button below the title bar of the Help window. Click the Next button to continue the list of questions.

7. To close the Help window, click the Close (X) button in the title bar.

TIP

Quick Help   For a definition or brief explanation of any screen in pcANYWHERE, press F1. Depending on where you are in the program, a Help box appears offering information about the screen, dialog box, or element in question. Press the Esc key or click anywhere on-screen to hide the Quick Help box.

USING THE CONTENTS HELP

You can find help on general topics by using the Contents tab of the Help Topics window. Topics such as frequently asked questions, tips and tricks, reference, and so on are collected together under one heading.

To use the Contents help, follow these steps:

1. Choose Help, Contents. The Help Topics window appears with the Contents tab displayed.

2. Double-click any topic preceded with a book icon to view related topics. Book icons represent topics; document icons represent the Help text (as shown in Figure 2.2).

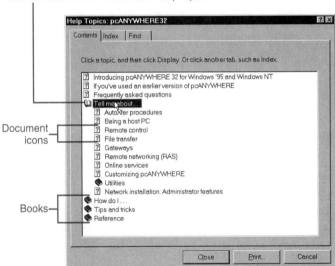

FIGURE 2.2   View the available help topics.

3. Double-click any document icon to view the text about that subject.

4. When viewing Help text, you can return to the Help Topics window at any time by clicking the Help Topics button below the title bar in the Help window.

5. Click any underlined term or phrase in the Help window to view a definition of the term (see Figure 2.3). Click anywhere else in the window to hide the definition.

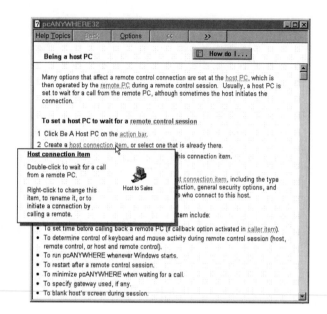

FIGURE 2.3   View definitions of underlined terms and phrases.

6. Click the How Do I button near the top of the Help windows to view a list of related topics. Double-click any topic in the list to view its Help screen.

7. To close the Help window, click the Close (X) button.

Want to Print a Topic?   To print any Help text, choose the Options button below the title bar and from the menu that appears, choose Print Topic.

USING THE HELP INDEX

You can use the Help Index to search for specific terms or procedures in pcANYWHERE. Find help on terms such as *modem, folders, calling, security,* and so on.

To use the Help Index, follow these steps:

1. Choose Help, Contents. The Help Topics dialog box appears.

2. Choose the Index tab. In the 1 text box, enter the term or phrase you want to search for, online for example.

3. The Index jumps to that term and displays available related topics, as shown in Figure 2.4.

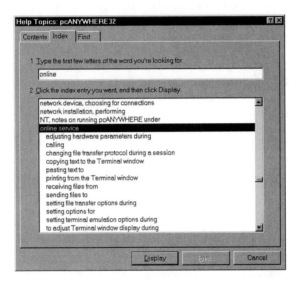

FIGURE 2.4   Scroll through available topics related to the word you entered.

4. Scroll the Help topics and select the one you want to view. Click the Display button; alternatively, double-click the Help topic you want to show. The Help window appears, displaying the text you requested.

5. You can click the Help Topics button to return to the Index tab of the Help Topics window; you can click the Back button to view the previously viewed Help window; or you can click the Close (X) button to close the Help window.

USING THE FIND FEATURE

pcANYWHERE's Help Topics window offers one more tab: the Find tab. Use the Find tab to search for topics, similarly to the Index tab; however, you can find words such as *about, never, terminates, clear,* and so on.

TIP   **Configure Find First**   Before you use the Find feature, you need to run the Find Setup Wizard that appears when you first choose the Find tab. Choose the Next button in the Wizard dialog box so Help can collect the terms for use in Help. Next, click the Finish button. The Find tab appears.

To use the Find tab, follow these steps:

1. Choose Help, Contents, and then select the Find tab. The first time you open the Find tab, you must run the Setup Wizard; follow the directions on-screen.

2. In the Find tab, enter the term for which you're searching in the 1 text box.

3. In the 2 list box, narrow the search by selecting one or more of the terms listed. To select multiple terms, select the first term, hold down the Ctrl key, and select the other terms you want to view (as shown in Figure 2.5).

4. In the 3 list, choose the topic you want to view and then click Display; alternatively, double-click the topic. The Help window appears.

5. View the topic and then choose one of the following:

   • Help Topics button to return to the Help Topics window.

   • Back button to go to the previously viewed Help window.

   • Close button to close the Help window.

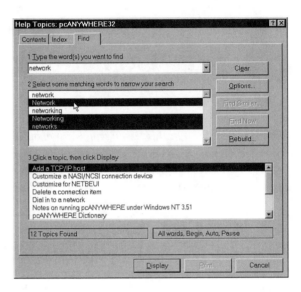

FIGURE 2.5 Use the Find tab to search for terms not necessarily listed in the Index list.

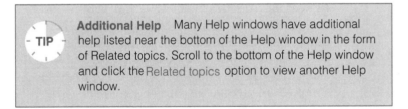

Additional Help Many Help windows have additional help listed near the bottom of the Help window in the form of Related topics. Scroll to the bottom of the Help window and click the Related topics option to view another Help window.

In this lesson, you learned how to use the program's Help feature. In the next lesson, you learn about pcANYWHERE's connections.

CONNECTION CONFIGURATIONS

In this lesson, you learn about the types of pcANYWHERE connections, create an example connection, and manage connections.

pcANYWHERE MODES

You can connect a computer using pcANYWHERE in various configurations. Your computer system setup governs how you want to connect. Appendix B describes the types of connections you can use. In conjunction with connection types, pcANYWHERE offers six modes of connections. Following is a summary of the six modes; each mode is described in detail in the coming lessons:

 Be A Host Use this mode when you want to answer requests from one or more remote computers. Computers can call your host computer to transfer files, remotely control your computer, and otherwise manipulate the host. You can set limits to what the remote computer can do with your computer; you also can set security options to limit access. See Lessons 9–12 for more information.

 Remote Control Use this mode to control a pcANY-WHERE host from a remote computer. You might want to use this mode, for example, from your home computer to your office computer. For more information, see Lessons 13–15.

 File Transfer This mode enables you to connect to a pcANYWHERE host computer and immediately transfer files. You might use this mode to transfer files from your laptop computer to the server computer at your office, for example, or to transfer files from the server to your laptop.

Be A Gateway   A gateway is a bridge between two computers on a network. The gateway enables users to share the modem, for example, on the gateway PC. For more information about being a gateway, see Lessons 20–21.

 Remote Networking   Use remote networking to connect to a network from a distance, yet enabling your remote PC to become a workstation on the network with access to network files and services. Use this feature when, for example, you want to connect to the network from an out-of-town road trip and transfer your expense account files to the server. For more information, see Lessons 7–8.

 Call Online Services   Online services provide you with information, news, forums, e-mail, and any number of services. When you call an online service, you're connected to the remote computer but you cannot control that computer in any way; the remote computer controls the session. For more information about online services, see Lessons 4–6.

CREATING A SAMPLE CONNECTION

To give you an idea of how connections work, you'll create a sample connection item. A connection item is a collection of files that define the information pcANYWHERE needs to make a connection to a remote computer, including information about the device (modem or network, for example) you use to make the connection and any commands or options you need to complete the connection. You'll learn more about connections throughout the book; for now, you'll create a connection item for being a host.

 Host   The computer that waits for a call from a remote computer and then supplies the remote computer with files, resources, or other items it requests. See Lesson 9 for more information about host computers.

To create a sample connection, follow these steps:

1. Click the Be a Host button on the Action bar. The Add Be
   A Host PC Item icon appears (see Figure 3.1).

Click the Action bar button.   Add connection item appears.

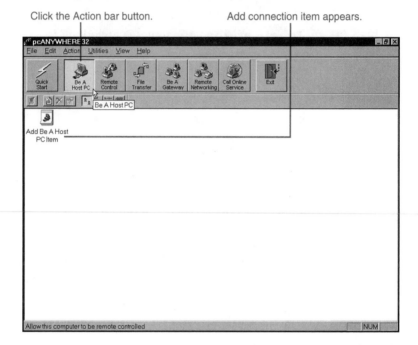

FIGURE 3.1   The Add Be A Host PC Item makes adding a connection item easy.

2. Double-click the Add Be A Host PC Item. The Be A Host
   PC Wizard dialog box appears.

3. In the first dialog box, enter a name for the host connection; you can enter **Sample** if you like. Click the Next
   button.

4. In the second wizard dialog box, a drop-down list of connection devices appears. For this sample, leave the default
   device as is and click the Next button.

Connection Devices   Any type of hardware you use for connecting to another computer, such as a modem, protocol, port, and so on.

5. In the third wizard dialog box, pcANYWHERE displays a check box that says, **Automatically Launch After Wizard**. Clear the check box by clicking it once to remove the check mark. Click the Finish button.

Figure 3.2 shows the connection item icon in the pcANYWHERE window. Note that the Sample connection item only displays when you click the Be A Host PC button in the Action bar.

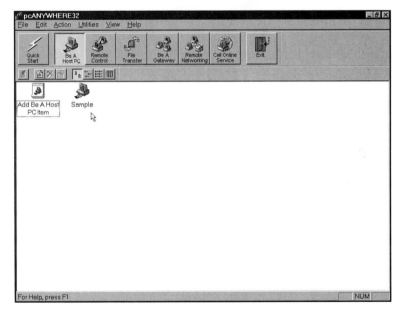

FIGURE 3.2   Add a connection item to the window for quick and easy connection.

Managing Connections

After you create connection items, you can double-click that item to use it. A remote connection item, such as you would create to attach to an online service, for example, would dial that service and connect to the remote computer when you double-click its connection item. A Be A Host connection item, on the other hand, would prepare your PC to receive a call from a remote computer. You'll learn more about creating and starting connection items in later lessons; however, for now, you'll learn to manage the connection item icons.

Managing a connection item includes such tasks as renaming, copying, and deleting the item, and viewing the item's properties.

Renaming a Connection Item

You might want to rename a connection item to organize your screen when you add new items. Renaming the item to make it more recognizable is also a possibility.

To rename a connection item, follow these steps:

1. Select the connection item.

2. Right-click the selected item and choose the Rename command from the quick menu.

3. The name under the item's icon changes to selected text within a box. Enter the new name and press Enter to accept it.

 TIP **Long, Descriptive Names** You can use names up to 255 characters to describe the item, if necessary.

COPYING A CONNECTION ITEM

You might want to copy a connection item as a base for another item, especially if the two items have similar configurations. After you paste the copied connection item, you can modify its properties as explained in the next section.

To copy a connection item, follow these steps:

1. Select the connection item.

2. Choose Edit, Copy.

3. Choose Edit, Paste. pcANYWHERE pastes the copy of the item and adds a number 1 to the name. You can rename the item if you want.

 TIP **Multiple Copies** You can paste the item again and again, as many times as you need to create the connection items you want. Just choose Edit, Paste to add another copy of the item.

VIEWING AN ITEM'S PROPERTIES

A connection item's properties include information about connection, settings, security options, and so on. You can view the properties and you can also modify the properties of a connection item.

Figure 3.3 shows the Sample Properties dialog box. Table 3.1 describes the tabs in the Sample's Properties dialog box. Each connection type displays a different set of tabs and options for modification. The properties displayed in the figure are for a host computer.

TABLE 3.1   PROPERTIES TABS

TAB	DESCRIPTION
Connection Info	Contains a list of devices the connection item uses (for more information about devices, see Appendix B).
Settings	Includes options for how pcANY-WHERE will manage the session; for example, for a host, the settings may include when to restart the host after the session, whether to use a screen saver while waiting for a call, and so on.
Callers	Enables you to specify the rights you want to grant to those who call your computer.
Security Options	Contains options for the connection, login, and session.
Protect Item	Enables you to use a password to protect the connection item.

To view a connection item's properties:

1. Select the item and choose File, Properties. The Sample Properties dialog box appears (see Figure 3.3).

2. Select the tab containing properties you want to view or modify.

3. If you make changes to one tab and then want to view another tab, click the Apply button to save the changes you've made before you change to another tab.

4. Click OK to close the Sample Properties dialog box.

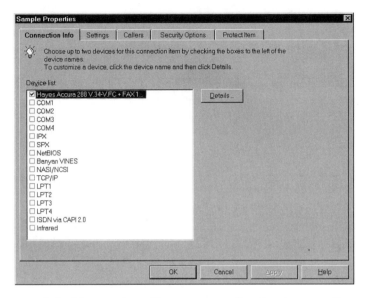

FIGURE 3.3 View and modify any connection item's properties.

DELETING A CONNECTION ITEM

You can delete a connection item when you no longer need it. To delete an item, do one of the following:

- Select the item and press the Delete key. Choose Yes in the confirmation dialog box displayed.

- Select the item and choose File, Delete. Confirm the deletion.

- Select the item and click the Delete Selected Items button on the Toolbar. Confirm the deletion.

- Right-click the selected item and choose Delete from the quick menu. Confirm the deletion.

In this lesson, you learned about the types of pcANYWHERE connections, created an example connection, and managed connections. In the next lesson, you learn about online services connections.

LESSON 4

CONFIGURING AN ONLINE SERVICE CONNECTION

In this lesson, you learn how to create a connection for online services, modify the connection, and configure connection options.

UNDERSTANDING AN ONLINE SERVICE CONNECTION

Connecting to an online service, such as CompuServe, MCI Mail, or another BBS, your computer acts as a remote PC, or a PC that is distant from the service. You use a modem and a phone line to connect to the service. You cannot, in any way, control the activities of the online service using your computer and pcANYWHERE.

You might want to connect to an online service to find information particular to the service, join others in a forum or discussion group, or to get technical help with a product or service you've received. A software BBS, for example, might advertise its new applications or upgrades, offer installation help over the BBS, and have a special area (forum) in which you can contact others who have used that software to discuss successes, problems, and so on.

 BBS (Electronic Bulletin Board Service) An online service run by an individual or company to advertise a product or service, supply a forum for interested parties, offer technical assistance, or perform some other service to customers, users, or just people calling in.

You use a connection item to connect to an online service; you can use a connection item that pcANYWHERE supplies, or you can create one. Since you'll likely need more than one connection item in your work, this lesson shows you how to create a connection item. Later, you can modify the existing item, if you feel the need.

A connection item is a collection of files that contain information about the connection, such as the device you use to make the connection (network, cable, modem) and any commands or options necessary to use during the session. The connection item, once it's configured, is represented by an icon and name and can be used over and over again after you create it.

You'll want to create one connection item for each online service you connect to; for example, create one connection item called CompuServe containing the specific configuration details necessary to connect to CompuServe; or create a connection item for a bulletin board you call for technical information.

CREATING THE CONNECTION

You can create connection items manually or you can use the Wizard pcANYWHERE supplies for quick and easy configuration. Either way, you must enter the name of the connection item, the device you'll use, and other details. If you use the Wizard to create the connection, you can edit the properties, just as you would if you created the connection item manually.

Wizard   A Wizard is a set of dialog boxes that guide you, step-by-step, to completing a task, such as creating a connection item. Wizards are easy to use and end in the same result as manual creation of an item would, but Wizards are easy to use, automatic, and effective.

To create an online service connection item, follow these steps:

1. Click the Call Online Service action button (see Figure 4.1). The Add Online Service Item icon appears.

Click here to start the Wizard.

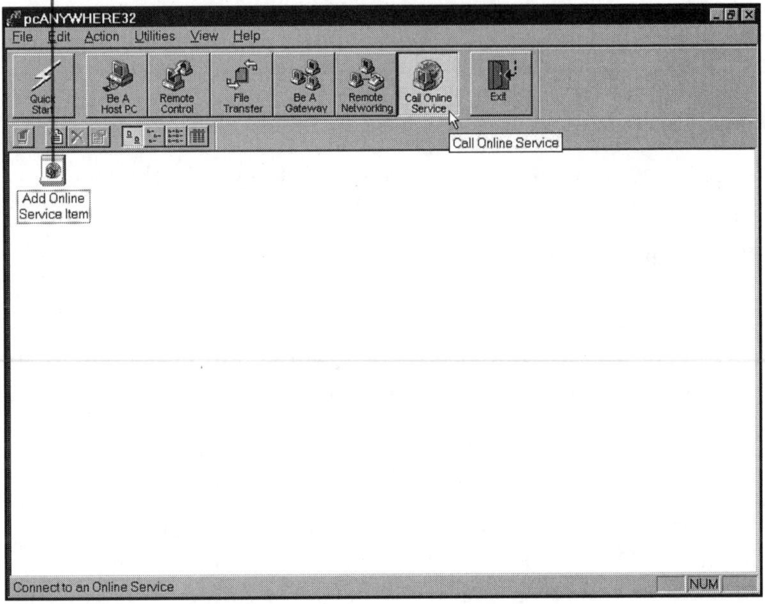

FIGURE 4.1   Click an action button to quickly perform a task.

2. Choose File, New; or double-click the Add Online Service Item icon. The Call an Online Service Wizard dialog box appears.

3. In the Type a Name for This Online Service Connection Item text box, enter a name and then click the Next button. The second Wizard dialog box appears.

4. In the Type of Device drop-down list box, choose the device type you'll use to connect to the service. For example, if you plan to use your modem and the phone lines, locate the name of your modem in the list and select it. Click the Next button.

TIP **What Types of Devices Are There?** For more information about types of devices, see Appendix B.

5. In the Online Service's Phone Number text box, enter the phone number of the service. Click the Next button.

6. In the Terminal Emulation drop-down list box, choose the terminal emulation for the service. You will need to contact the online service or find this information in the documentation for the service to be sure you have the right terminal emulation. Click Next.

Terminal Emulation A terminal is a device consisting of a monitor, video adapter, and keyboard that does no processing on its own. Instead, it's connected to a mainframe computer which does all processing for it; a terminal can only monitor and receive information from the mainframe, not store information. Since a PC can perform processing and can store information, it cannot communicate with a mainframe in the same way; therefore, pcANYWHERE emulates, or mimics, a terminal to connect and communicate with the computer on the other end of your online service.

7. If you want to connect to the online service as soon as you're finished with the Wizard, make sure there is a check mark in the Automatically Call the Online Service check box. Choose the Finish button. pcANYWHERE adds an icon with the name you specified under it to the screen to represent the new connection you created.

TIP **Easily Open a Connection** To open a connection item at any time after you create it, you can double-click the item's icon in the pcANYWHERE window.

MODIFYING THE CONNECTION

You can modify a connection item at any time to change connection information, settings, and other options. You can even add a password to the connection item to prevent others from using or modifying the connection from your PC.

To modify a connection, follow these steps:

1. In the Online Service window, select the online service you want to modify.

2. Choose File, Properties; alternatively, right-click the connection item and choose Properties from the shortcut menu. The connection's Properties dialog box appears (see Figure 4.2).

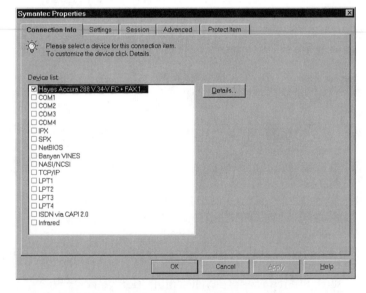

FIGURE 4.2 Customize the connection item's settings.

3. Make any changes to the settings as outlined in the following sections.

4. When you're finished making changes in one tab, click the Apply button to save those changes before choosing another tab to configure, or choose OK to close the dialog box.

Connection Info

Use the Connection Info tab (refer to Figure 4.2) to choose the communications device to use for the connection and then set the properties for that device. If, for example, you plan to attach to the online service over a network, you would use one of the protocols such as IPX, NetBIOS, or TCP/IP, as a device. For the most part, however, you connect to an online service by way of a modem.

After checking the box in front of the device in the Device List, click the Details button to display the Properties dialog box of the selected device. Properties you could modify for a modem, for example, include the port, speed, data and stop bits, and terminal window controls.

Settings Tab

Use the Settings tab to set terminal emulation, file transfer protocol, and the phone number settings for the online service. Figure 4.3 shows the Settings tab of the Properties dialog box.

The terminal emulation drop-down box enables your PC to communicate with other computers, such as a mainframe or minicomputer. Choose ANSI, WYSE 50, VT220, or other emulation as directed by the online service.

The file transfer protocol defines the rules by which the two computers communicate. You can choose zmodem, ymodem, kermit, ASCII, and so on. The online service will define the protocol you should use.

Use the Phone Number of Online Service area to define the number and any dialing properties for the connection item. Dialing properties include any information you need to access an outside line, use a calling card for dialing, disable call waiting, and so on. You also can set the number of redial attempts and number of seconds between redials in this area of the dialog box.

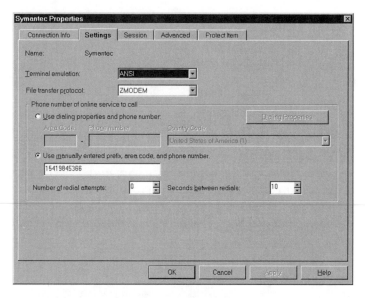

FIGURE 4.3 Configure settings such as phone number and dialing properties for the connection item.

SESSION TAB

Use the Session tab to configure options that apply to the online session, such as recording a session in a log, running script files, and so on. Figure 4.4 shows the Session tab of the Properties dialog box.

You can choose to record a session in a file so you can play it back later; this enables you to save everything that was displayed on-screen to a file. Check the Record Session in File for Later Playback check box and enter a drive, directory, and file name in which to save the file. You can click the Browse button to choose the path for the file.

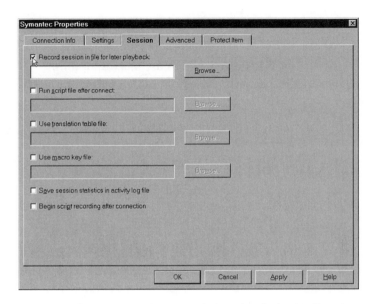

FIGURE 4.4   Set any tracking or scripting details in the Session tab.

Logging   pcANYWHERE can record a log, or text file, describing the events occurring during a session. You can later view the log to troubleshoot problems or errors, for example, or to review information you viewed on screen during the session.

Script   A program that executes when the user logs on to the service; scripts usually send user identification the service requires before granting access to the service.

Run Script File After Connect enables you to specify a script file that will automatically log you on to the service after connection. Check the option's box and enter the path and file name of an existing script file.

Use Translation Table File enables you to specify the use of a code that allows data to be converted from one format to another.

Use this option if you're transferring files during the session that are in different formats.

Use Macro Key File enables you to use macros, or mini-programs, to perform tasks during the online session. Save your macros to a file and then enter the path and file name in this text box.

The **Save Session Statistics in an Activity Log File** check box is used to record a session log of connection details for later review. **Check the Begin Script Recording After Connection** can be used to create a script file from your session.

ADVANCED TAB

Use the Advanced tab to set options that override the default values for terminal emulation. You might want to use these options, for example, if you want to use different configurations for one or two specific sessions. You can easily return to the default settings by clicking the Defaults button at any time.

Line Wrap defines how the lines of text display in the terminal window. Wrapping makes the text jump to the next line if it exceeds the width of the window.

Screen Wrap makes the text begin at the top of the screen again when the screen is filled. New text overwrites the current text on-screen.

Destructive <BS> Key causes the backspace key to delete a character to its right instead of to its left.

Translate Receive CR to CR/LF causes the cursor to move to the left of the window and advance one line when a carriage return character is received.

Break Length specifies the length of the signal used to interrupt programs running on a mainframe or minicomputer.

PROTECT ITEM TAB

Use to set a password that limits access to the connection item; only someone with the password can execute or modify the item. Figure 4.5 shows the Protect Item tab with a password entered.

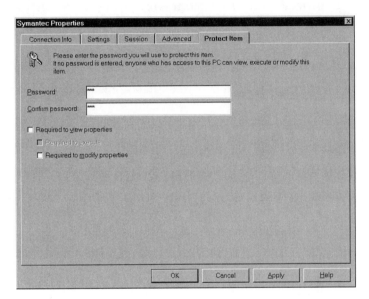

FIGURE 4.5 Protect the connection item from use by others.

To protect the item, enter a password and then enter the password a second time in the Confirm Password text box. You can also choose the following options:

> **Required to View Password** If you check this option, the user must know the password before she or he can view the connection item's Properties dialog box. If you choose this option, the Required to Execute option appears. Also, choosing this option automatically chooses the Required to Modify Properties check box.

Required to Execute   Appears only if you check the Required to View Password check box; check this option to prevent anyone who does not know the password from using the connection item to attach to the service.

Required to Modify Properties   If you do not choose to limit the viewing of the properties, you can choose this option to limit modification of the properties to only those users with the password.

In this lesson, you learned how to create a connection for online services, modify the connection, and configure connection options. In the next lesson, you learn to run an online service session.

RUNNING AN ONLINE SERVICE SESSION

In this lesson, you learn to start a session, manage a session, and print a session.

STARTING THE SESSION

You can initiate a session with an online service by double-clicking the connection item in the Call Online Service window of pcANYWHERE. pcANYWHERE dials the specified number and connects with the remote host.

Each service has its own procedures, log in, and security measures. With pcANYWHERE, your PC emulates the terminal type and uses file-transfer protocols that the online service needs in order to communicate with you. You'll need to first contact the online service to find out what terminal type and protocol it requires.

Where's pcANYWHERE? While pcANYWHERE is dialing and connecting to the online service, the pcANYWHERE window disappears from the screen. When you disconnect from the service; however, the pcANYWHERE screen will reappear.

Make sure your modem is turned on, then follow these steps:

1. Choose the Call Online Service action button and select the connection item.

2. Choose Action, Connect, or right-click the selected item and choose Connect from the shortcut menu; alternatively, double-click the connection item. A connection dialog box appears while pcANYWHERE dials the number.

3. When the connection is successful, the terminal window appears; an example is shown in Figure 5.1.

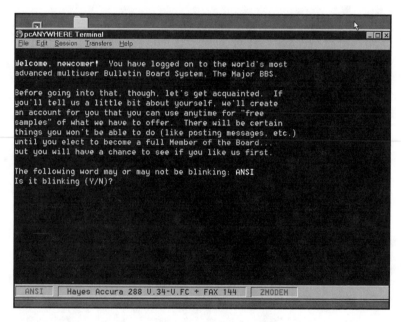

Figure 5.1   Follow the directions on-screen.

Managing the Session

After you connect and the terminal window appears. It is in the terminal window that you control the session. Most online services, bulletin boards, and other services using a terminal window make it easy for you to access their services by listing instructions, steps, menus, and other methods of help. In most cases, you don't need to know any special commands or languages to use terminal mode. Most services display choices and directions for accessing libraries, files, and forums.

Additionally, you can use the pcANYWHERE Terminal menu bar to control the session. The menu items enable you to perform activities such as printing, sending and receiving files, and so on. Following is a summary of what each menu enables you to do:

File   Save the screen to a file name, record a script, print the screen, exit the terminal window.

Edit   Paste selected text. Copy or cut text from another Windows application and then in the terminal window, choose Edit, Paste to place the text in the local terminal window; choose Edit, Paste to Host to send the text to the online service.

Session   Reset the terminal, change to monitor mode, change settings for the terminal and the display, and so on. Terminal settings include emulation, font and colors, line wrap, screen wrap, and so on. Display settings include automatic font sizing, scroll bars, and the like.

Transfers   Send and receive files, change protocols. See Lesson 6, "Transferring Files from an Online Service" for more information.

Help   Get help about working with a terminal.

Using Scripts to Automate the Session   If you want to try your hand at writing scripts, see the book *Creating Scripts* that comes with pcANYWHERE. You can use scripts to automate your session, making the time spent online more efficient.

PRINTING FROM THE SESSION

If you need to record the information on-screen during an online session, you can print the screen text for a quick record of the session.

You also can change the printer setup during a session to change page size or orientation.

PRINTING

You can choose to print one screen or to print continuously during the session.

To print one screen from the session, follow these steps:

1. With the screen you want to print displayed, choose File, Print Screen. The confirmation dialog box appears.

2. Choose Yes to print. pcANYWHERE sends the job to your printer.

To print continuously throughout the session, choose Sessions, Print Online. Each screen during the session is printed. To end continuous printing, choose Sessions, Print Online again to turn the command off.

PRINT SETUP

You can change the printer setup by modifying the page size and source, the orientation of the page printed, and making other changes in the Print Setup dialog box.

To change the printer setup, follow these steps:

1. Choose File, Print Setup. The Print Setup dialog box appears (see Figure 5.2).

2. Choose the printer you want to configure in the Printer area of the dialog box, from the Name drop-down list box.

3. To change printer settings, click the Properties button. Make any changes to paper size, graphics resolution, fonts, or other options; choose OK when done.

4. In the Paper area of the dialog box, choose the paper size and the source.

5. In the Orientation area of the dialog box, choose either Portrait or Landscape.

6. Choose OK to close the Print Setup dialog box.

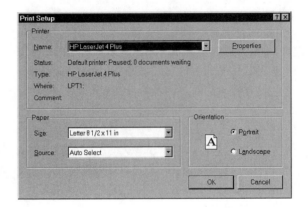

FIGURE 5.2 Change the print setup for printing from a terminal window.

ENDING A SESSION

Many services provide menus telling you how to log off or exit the system (see Figure 5.3). If you don't follow the service's directions, it may think you're still connected and cause problems the next time you try to connect. When you exit the service using the service's exit command, pcANYWHERE disconnects from the service, closes the terminal window, and returns to the pcANYWHERE window.

If you cannot find a command, menu, or other directions for exiting a service, choose File, Exit. pcANYWHERE will disconnect from the service and return to the pcANYWHERE window.

In this lesson, you learned to start a session, manage a session, and print a session. In the next lesson, you learn to transfer files from an online service.

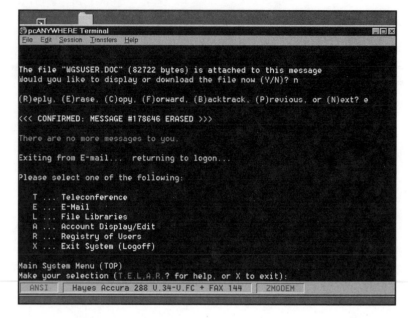

FIGURE 5.3   Exit the service.

TRANSFERRING FILES FROM AN ONLINE SERVICE

6

In this lesson, you learn to upload and download files during a session with an online service or BBS.

UNDERSTANDING PROTOCOLS

You can send and receive files through an online service or bulletin board as long as you and the service are using the same file-transfer protocol. Most services let you specify the protocol from a list of available protocols the service can use. Alternatively, you can specify the protocol you want to use during the session from within pcANYWHERE.

 Protocol The formal specification that defines the procedures to follow when transmitting and receiving data. Protocols define the format, timing, sequence, and error checking used by the communications software.

pcANYWHERE offers several popular file-transfer protocols. Following is a list of the basic protocols; pcANYWHERE includes some variations of the Xmodem and Ymodem protocols that perform special error-checking or file transfer services. Make sure you check with the online service to see which protocols they support before choosing one of the following:

Xmodem   A popular and easily-obtainable protocol which divides the data for transmission into blocks; each block consists of the start-of-header character, a block number, 128 bytes of data and a checksum.

Xmodem-CRC   Adds more stringent error-checking—cyclical redundancy check—to detect transmission errors to the Xmodem protocol.

Ymodem   A variation of the Xmodem protocol, Ymodem divides the data into blocks that consist of the start-of-header character, a block number, 1 kilobyte of data, and the checksum. Using Ymodem results in less overhead for error control than required by Xmodem; however, if the block must be retransmitted because the protocol detects an error, there is more data to resend.

Zmodem   Similar to Xmodem and Ymodem, Zmodem is designed to handle larger data transfers with fewer errors. Zmodem also contains a feature called checkpoint restart, which allows an interrupted transmission to resume at the point of interruption, rather than starting again at the beginning of the transmission.

Kermit   Transmits data in variable-length blocks up to 96 characters long, and each block is checked for transmission errors. If errors are detected, Kermit initiates repeat transmissions automatically.

ASCII Is a File Type, Not a Protocol   ASCII (American Standard Code for Information Interchange) is a standard coding scheme that assigns numeric values to letters, numbers, and other characters to achieve compatibility among different computers and peripheral devices.

Establish a Default Protocol   If there is a service you often use and you want to establish a default protocol for that service, you can add the information to the Settings tab in the connection item's Property dialog box (see Lesson 4, "Configuring an Online Service Connection").

You can change a protocol in the terminal window during a session using the following pcANYWHERE feature. Follow these steps:

1. In the terminal window, choose Transfers, Protocol. The File Transfer Protocol dialog box appears (see Figure 6.1).

FIGURE 6.1   Choose a protocol for the current session.

2. Choose the protocol you want to use and choose OK.

UPLOADING FILES

When you upload a file, you're sending that file to the online service using a file transfer protocol that's acceptable to your computer and to the service's computer. You can follow the on-screen instructions displayed by the service to successfully upload files or you can use pcANYWHERE features to perform the same task.

USING THE ONLINE SERVICE TO UPLOAD FILES

Most services provide a menu system that you can use to locate the area to which you will upload files. Figure 6.2 shows a menu system that enables you to upload files to a File Library.

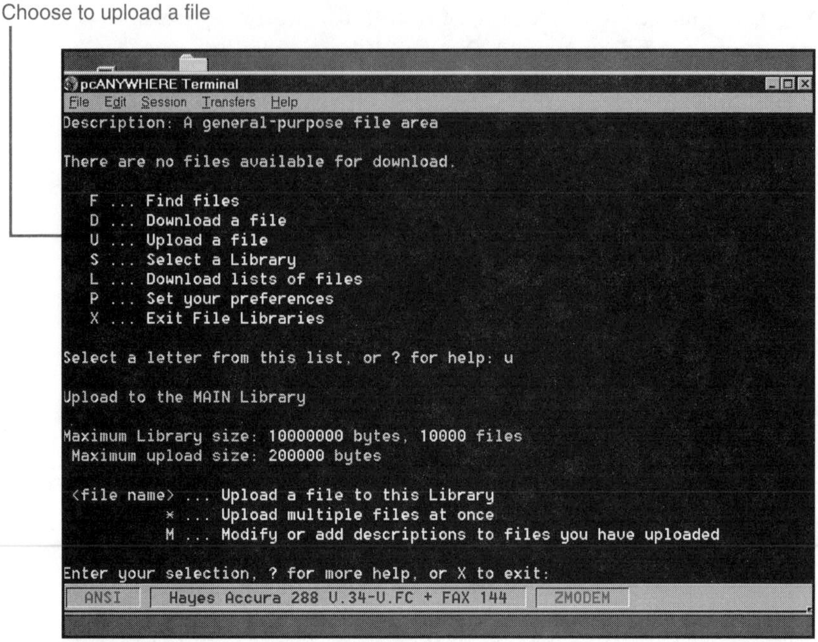

Choose to upload a file

```
pcANYWHERE Terminal                                          _ □ ✕
File  Edit  Session  Transfers  Help
Description: A general-purpose file area

There are no files available for download.

    F ... Find files
    D ... Download a file
    U ... Upload a file
    S ... Select a Library
    L ... Download lists of files
    P ... Set your preferences
    X ... Exit File Libraries

Select a letter from this list, or ? for help: u

Upload to the MAIN Library

Maximum Library size: 10000000 bytes, 10000 files
 Maximum upload size: 200000 bytes

<file name> ... Upload a file to this Library
         * ... Upload multiple files at once
         M ... Modify or add descriptions to files you have uploaded

Enter your selection, ? for more help, or X to exit:
 ANSI    Hayes Accura 288 V.34-V.FC + FAX 144    ZMODEM
```

FIGURE 6.2   Use the online service's menu to upload a file.

The service will ask you for the file name you want to upload. You should also include the path to that file on your drive. Next, the service will ask for the protocol you want to use (see Figure 6.3).

pcANYWHERE uploads the file for you and when finished, it returns to the online service's menu.

USING pcANYWHERE TO UPLOAD FILES

The only difference between the two methods is that when using pcANYWHERE's feature, you can choose the file from your hard drive by browsing the drive instead of remembering the file name.

To upload a file to an online service, you can follow these steps:

1. After connecting to the service, choose Transfer, Send File.

2. The Select Files to Send dialog box appears (see Figure 6.4).

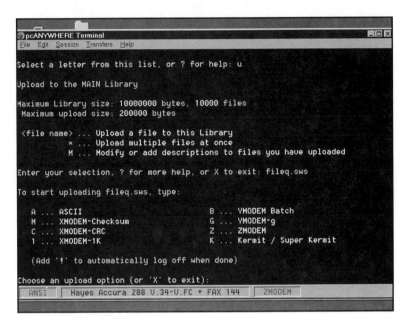

FIGURE 6.3 Choose the most convenient protocol for your file.

3. Choose the file you want to upload.

4. Choose OK. pcANYWHERE transfers the file to the online service.

DOWNLOADING A FILE

Downloading files is the same as receiving files. Again, the two computers must use the same protocol to transfer the files. When you download a file using pcANYWHERE, the file is, by default, placed in the pcANYWHERE program folder; you can, however, change that default by specifying a target folder.

FIGURE 6.4 Select the file to send.

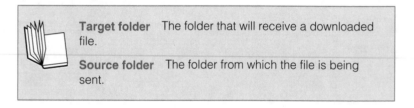

Target folder   The folder that will receive a downloaded file.

Source folder   The folder from which the file is being sent.

Using the menu supplied by the online service, you'll want to locate the file for downloading. You may look in a library, index, or other listing of files, as displayed in the service's menu.

Next, you may need to find the file name, if you don't already know it. Most services offer a file search feature in which you can enter a keyword, a date, partial file name, or other criteria (see Figure 6.5). Often, you can mark, or tag, the file(s) in some manner when you've found the one(s) you want.

Finally, you'll need to list the file(s) to download and then choose the protocol, as shown in Figure 6.6. pcANYWHERE will prompt you to enter a location on your hard drive in which to place the file and then download the file for you.

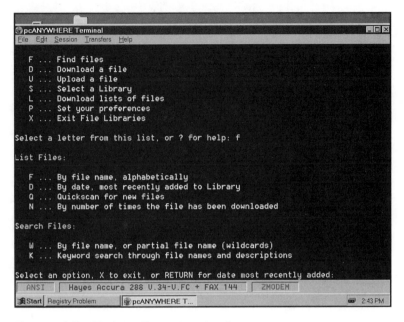

FIGURE 6.5   Find the file to download.

As an alternative to the previous procedure, you can follow these steps to downloading a file:

1. After connecting to the service, select the file from the service using the service's instructions.

2. Choose Transfer, Receive File. The Select File to Receive dialog box appears.

3. Choose the drive and folder to which you want to send the downloaded file and choose OK. The file is transferred.

FIGURE 6.6 Choose the protocol to download.

In this lesson, you learned to upload and download files during a session with an online service or BBS. In the next lesson, you learn to configure a remote network connection.

Configuring a Remote Network Connection

In this lesson, you learn to create a remote network connection and modify it.

Understanding Remote Network Connections

You use remote networking when you want to connect to a network as a workstation, or network node. Suppose you're working from home or on the road. You can connect your PC to the dial-up server on the network at the office to access network files and services.

Normally, network connections between workstations and servers are made through a cable and the connected PCs are generally in the same office or building. A connection such as this is called a LAN, or local area network. PCs in a LAN can access files, directories, printers, and other shared resources for which the user has permission to access.

Similarly, a workstation connected to a network remotely can access any file or resource for which the user has permission to access. When you need to access a file, for example, you can go to the appropriate network drive and copy, print, or open the file, just as you would if you were attached to the network via a LAN.

TIP   **Computer to Computer**   pcANYWHERE must be in-stalled on both computers—the remote computer and the office computer—to perform a remote network connection.

Applications are executed on the remote PC and any data required by the application is communicated over the telephone lines to the remote PC. For example, say you're working with an accounting program and remote networking from home. The program itself is located and running on your PC's hard drive. Data you need to complete a report, however, may be located on the server at the office. When the accounting program requests the data it needs, pcANYWHERE sends the request over the phone lines to the server and the server sends the data back over the phone lines to your PC and the accounting program.

Slow Connection?   When you're working with remote networking, you must remember that telephone lines are much slower than direct LAN connections, even if you're using a high-speed modem.

CREATING A REMOTE NETWORK CONNECTION

Creating a remote network connection consists of entering an item's name and the connection device it will use, along with other configuration settings that enable the connection to take place. pcANYWHERE includes a Wizard to help you create a connection item.

After you create the connection, you can activate it to have pcANYWHERE dial the dial-up networking server; then you can log on to the network.

Follow these steps to create a remote network connection:

1. In the Action bar, click the Remote Networking action button.

2. Choose File, New or double-click the Add Remote Networking Item icon (see Figure 7.1).

 No Remote Networking Action Button?   If the Remote Networking action button is dimmed, you'll have to install Dial-Up Networking in Windows 95 or Remote Access Service (RAS) in Windows NT before you can create a remote connection. See your Windows online Help or documentation for more information.

Remote Networking action button

FIGURE 7.1   Use the Wizard to add the connection item.

3. In the first Wizard dialog box, enter a name for the connection item (generally you use the name of the dial-up computer on the network). Figure 7.2 shows the first Wizard dialog box.

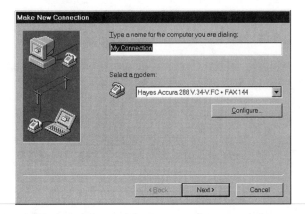

Figure 7.2 Enter a name for the connection item and select your modem.

4. Select a modem to use for the connection; if you only have one modem connected to your computer, that modem will display in the Select a Modem text box. Click the Next button.

 No Modem Listed? If no modem appears in the text box, you must first install a modem through the Windows Control Panel.

 TIP **Last Minute Configuration** Click the Configure button to make any changes to the modem's configuration—including speaker volume, port, and call preferences.

5. In the second Wizard dialog box, enter the area code and phone number of the computer you are calling. Check to make sure the country code is correct. Click Next.

6. The last Wizard dialog box informs you the item was successfully created. Click Finish to close the Wizard. The item appears in the Remote Networking window.

MODIFYING A REMOTE NETWORK CONNECTION

You can modify the connection item's properties at any time, by changing the phone number or the modem you use for the connection. Additionally, you can change the modem's properties for use with the specific network connection (see Figure 7.3).

To modify a remote network connection, follow these steps:

1. In the Remote Networking window of pcANYWHERE, select the connection you want to modify.

2. Choose File, Properties; alternatively, right-click the item and choose Properties from the shortcut menu.

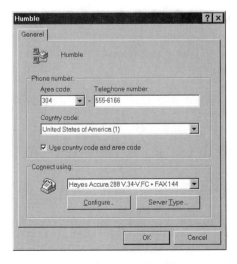

FIGURE 7.3 Make changes in the connection item's properties dialog box.

3. In the properties dialog box, make any changes to the phone number, area code, or country code.

4. To change the modem, click the down arrow beside the Connect Using text box and select a new modem.

5. To configure the modem, click the Configure button.

6. To set specific data about the server, click the Server Types button. If you need help with choosing server options, see your network administrator. Figure 7.4 displays the Server Types dialog box and Table 7.1 describes the options in the dialog box.

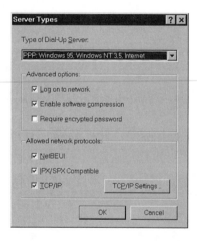

FIGURE 7.4   Set server-specific options in the Server Types dialog box.

7. Choose OK to close the Server Types dialog box. Choose OK to close the connection item's properties dialog box.

TABLE 7.1   SERVER TYPES OPTIONS

OPTION	DESCRIPTION
Type of Dial-Up Server	Lists the server types: NetWare, Windows 95 or NT 4, Windows for Workgroups, and so on.

OPTION	DESCRIPTION
Advanced Options Area	
Log on to Network	Logs onto the network using the username and password you entered when you logged into Windows.
Enable Software Compression	Enables compression of incoming and outgoing data and therefore speeds the transfer; the computer to which you are sending the data must be able to compress data for this option to work.
Require Encrypted Password	Adds the security of encrypted passwords; the computer you're dialing must also support encrypted passwords for this option to work.
Allowed Network Protocols Area	
	Choose NetBEUI, IPX/SPX Compatible, TCP/IP, or a combination of the three.
TCP/IP Settings	Defines your IP address, the server's DNS address, and other information needed for you to use TCP/IP.

NRN   In the Type of Dial-Up Servers drop-down list, NRN describes a connection to a NetWare server configured for dial-up networking.

PPP   Point-to-Point Protocol; a protocol that provides host-to-network connections over synchronous and asynchronous links. Choose this option in the Type of Dial-Up Server drop-down list if you're connecting to the Internet.

In this lesson, you learned to create a remote network connection and modify it. In the next lesson, you learn to run a remote network session.

8

RUNNING A REMOTE NETWORK SESSION

In this lesson, you learn how to connect to the network, access files and resources, and end the connection.

CONNECTING TO THE NETWORK

pcANYWHERE creates the remote network connection using the information you entered in the connection item's property page (refer to Lesson 7). When you connect to the server, you must log in with a valid user name and password. Also, you'll want to check with your network administrator to make sure you have permission to dial in and connect to the network. After logging in to the network, you can access drives, files, directories, and other resources for which you have permission.

To connect to the network remotely, follow these steps:

1. In the Remote Networking window of pcANYWHERE, select the connection item and choose Action, Connect; alternatively, right-click the item and choose Connect from the shortcut menu. Or you can double-click the item to connect.

Permission from the Host This provides guidance for setting up connections and running sessions from the host computer. Lesson 10 explains how to set control and access permissions for the remote caller.

2. The Dial-Up Networking dialog box appears (see Figure
8.1). You can choose whether to exert remote control
over the computer you're dialing, if you have permission. If you choose remote control, you'll need to set
the remote access properties; for more information,
see Lesson 13.

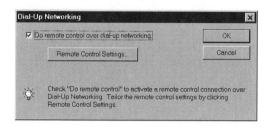

FIGURE 8.1   Choose whether to remote control the computer
you're dialing.

3. Choose OK to continue. pcANYWHERE dials and then
connects to the host computer; if your speaker is turned
up, you can hear the handshake between modems.

Handshake   The exchange of characters, or codes, to
maintain and coordinate data flow between the two modems, so that data is transmitted only when the receiving
modem is ready to accept the data.

4. The Logon dialog box appears, as shown in Figure 8.2.
Enter your user name, password, domain, and any other
information requested. Choose OK to continue.

5. The connection dialog box displays the words: **Server
authenticating**. When the host PC confirms your user
identification, it logs you onto the network and then
returns to pcANYWHERE.

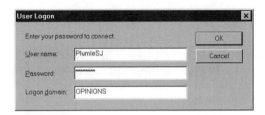

FIGURE 8.2   Enter your user name, password, or other information if prompted.

On the Taskbar, you'll notice the minimized Connection dialog box. You can switch to that box to view details about your connection to the network. Click the Details button to view more information.

ACCESSING FILES AND RESOURCES

Methods for accessing files and resources depend on the host PC, the network type, and the applications you're using on your PC. You should be able to access files and directories, print through the host to a network printer, and access other resources, as well.

In this section, I'll show you a couple of examples for accessing files after connecting.

MAPPING A NETWORK DRIVE

You can access the network through an application that requires you to map a network drive. When you map a drive, you access the directory, subdirectory, and file you want from the server; mapping provides a convenient shortcut to that file.

Map a Drive   Assigning a drive letter to a directory path; for example, drive F: could be mapped to the server\ directory\subdirectory: \\Humble\MSOffice\Winword\.

Suppose you're using an application on your PC but you want to open a file from the network through your remote connection. In the application you can, for example, choose File, Open to display the Open dialog box. Then access the file by clicking the Network button, if available, in the dialog box; if no Network button is available, you can attach through the Explorer. Figure 8.3 shows the Map Network Drive dialog box that appears.

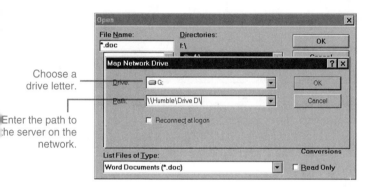

FIGURE 8.3   Some applications enable you to map a network drive to access files.

Some applications enable you to map drives from other dialog boxes, such as the Save As dialog box or a search of file finding dialog box. When you see a button with "Network" on it, that usually leads you to the Map Network Drive dialog box.

ACCESSING FILES THROUGH THE NETWORK NEIGHBORHOOD

By opening the Network Neighborhood, you can access the server and any drives, directories, and files for which you have permission. Double-click the Network Neighborhood to open the network connection. Figure 8.4 shows the server's window and available folders.

FIGURE 8.4   Access directories and files as you normally would through the Network Neighborhood.

PRINTING OVER THE NETWORK

To use a printer over the network, you must first install the printer drivers to your remote PC. You install a network printer using the Add Printer Wizard in the Printers folder.

Choose Start, Settings, Printers and then double-click the Add Printer Wizard. Click Next in the first Wizard dialog box to install the printer. In the second Wizard dialog box, choose the Network Printer option and then click Next.

In the next Wizard dialog box, enter the network path to the printer you want to install; you can alternatively use the Browse button. Figure 8.5 shows the Browse for Printer dialog box with the printer selected under the network server. Choose OK to continue.

Follow the directions in the Wizard dialog boxes. You'll choose the manufacturer and model of the printer, assign a printer name, and so on. When you're done, Windows adds the network printer to your Printer folder and you can access that printer from your Windows applications (see Figure 8.6).

FIGURE 8.5   Add the network printer driver to your hard drive.

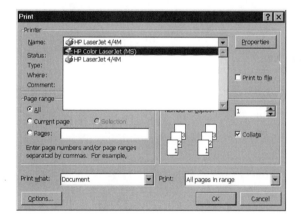

FIGURE 8.6   Access the network printer from your applications.

Naturally, before you print, you must be connected to the network and when you print to the network printer, your job will be printed out at work instead of at your remote location.

Ending the Connection

When you're finished working with the remote connection, you can end the connection.

To disconnect, use the taskbar to display the Connected to dialog box. Click the Disconnect button. pcANYWHERE closes the connection.

In this lesson, you learned how to connect to the network, access files and resources, and end the connection. In the next lesson, you learn to configure a host connection.

CONFIGURING HOST CONNECTIONS

In this lesson, you learn how to create a host connection item and modify the host connection.

UNDERSTANDING A HOST CONNECTION

You create a host connection item, or you may be a host, when you want remote PCs to have access to your computer. You may want to share files with a user that is on the road or enable a colleague that is at home sick to print a report from your computer.

In addition to using the resources on your PC, users could connect to your host PC to access network resources, if they have permission to use those resources. You can install pcANYWHERE on the network server, for example, to enable remote access to the network's resources.

When you open a host window, you're enabling pcANYWHERE to answer a call, cable connection, or network connection that will access your computer's resources. When you become a host PC using pcANYWHERE, you can configure your PC to protect your files and resources and to minimize what you see on the host as others are accessing it.

CREATING A HOST CONNECTION

pcANYWHERE includes three default host connection icons you can use or you can create your own connection item. When you create your own connection item, you use the Add Be A Host PC Item icon to configure the connection to suit your own purposes.

Alternatively, you can use one of pcANYWHERE's default items. If you use a default item, you can modify any of the item's settings, as described in the next section. Following is a description of the three default host connection items in pcANYWHERE:

DIRECT   Use this icon to open a Host window for a direct cable connection on LPT1. This item enables full access to all callers, limited security options, and no password protection.

MODEM   Use this icon to open a Host window for a modem connection using the default modem attached to your computer. This item also enables full access to all callers, little security, and no password protection.

NETWORK   Use this item to open a Host window for a network connection using the default network protocol, full access to all requests, little security, and no password protection.

To create a host connection, follow these steps:

1. Click the Be A Host PC button in the Action bar. The Be A Host PC window appears (see Figure 9.1).

2. Double-click the Be A Host PC Wizard to create a connection item from scratch; alternatively, select an existing item and skip to the next section, "Modifying the Host Connection."

3. Enter the name of the connection item in the first Wizard dialog box; click the Next button to continue.

4. In the second Wizard dialog box, choose the connection device—modem, COM port, protocol, or other device—and click Next.

5. In the final Wizard dialog box, choose whether to launch the item immediately and click the Finish button. If you

clear the Automatically Launch After Wizard check box,
the item will not start when you close the Wizard.

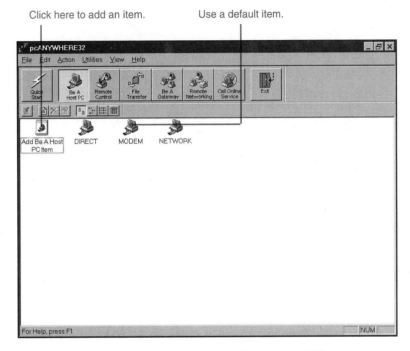

FIGURE 9.1   Click Be A Host PC to enable remote PCs to access
your resources.

When you're done, pcANYWHERE adds the new connection item
to the Be A Host PC window. If you chose to automatically launch
the item, pcANYWHERE closes, leaving a minimized
pcANYWHERE Waiting dialog box; this item remains in the background, waiting for a call, until you Cancel the dialog box. If you
cancel the dialog box, pcANYWHERE closes the connection item
and returns to the pcANYWHERE window. Figure 9.2 shows the
restored pcANYWHERE Waiting dialog box.

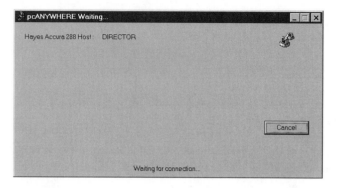

FIGURE 9.2   The launched connection item waits for a call.

MODIFYING THE HOST CONNECTION

Whether you've created a new host connection item or you're modifying the properties of an existing host connection item, you can change settings and options to customize the item to your needs.

Included in the settings you can modify are device names and details and various other settings. This section shows you how to modify these settings for a host connection; Lessons 10 and 11 show you how to configure callers and set security options for the host connection item.

CONNECTION INFO

Connection Info refers to the device you're using for the host connection item and any specific configuration options that relate to that item. For a host connection item, you can choose one or two devices to associate with the item. If you choose a modem and protocol, for example, the host connection item will answer a request from either device. You can use the following connection information for setting the host to wait for a call or for configuring the host to call the remote.

To modify a host connection, follow these steps:

1. In the Be A Host PC window, select the host connection item you want to modify and choose File, Properties; alternatively, right-click the item and choose Properties from the shortcut menu. The host item's Properties dialog box appears.

2. To select a device or modify device settings, choose the Connection Info tab, shown in Figure 9.3.

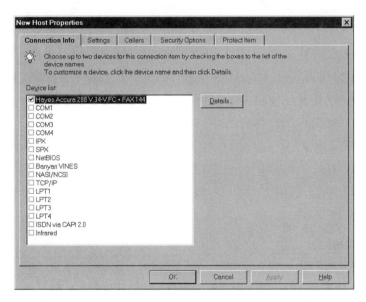

Figure 9.3 Choose the device for the connection item.

3. Check the box beside one or two devices in the Device list.

4. To configure a device, select the device in the Device List and then click the Details button. A Properties dialog box appears containing settings you can modify that are specific to the selected device; for example, a modem's properties include port, speed, speaker volume, and so on.

Details Button Dimmed?   If you select a device and the Details button is dimmed, you must first install the device to Windows before you can configure it.

5. Choose OK to accept the changes and close the dialog box; however, if you want to make more changes to other tabs in the dialog box, click the Apply button to save the changes to the Connection Info tab, then click the appropriate tabs (as described below) to make further changes.

SETTINGS

The Settings tab contains options you can choose that refer to the host's actions. Figure 9.4 shows the Settings tab and Table 9.1 describes the options in the Settings tab of the Properties dialog box.

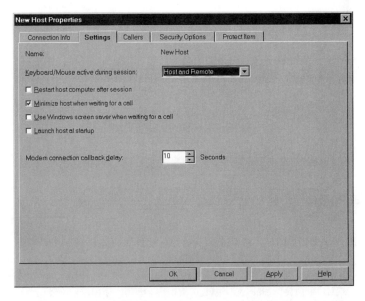

FIGURE 9.4   Use the Settings tab to control the host connection item.

TABLE 9.1 SETTINGS OPTIONS

OPTION	DESCRIPTION
Keyboard/Mouse Active During Session	Host and Remote enables keyboard and mouse activity by both computers; Host means only the host PC has control over the keyboard and mouse of both PCs; and Remote means only the remote PC has control over the keyboard and mouse of both PCs.
Restart Host When Waiting for a Call	A checked box means the host PC restarts after every session or abnormal disconnection; not recommended if the host is also a server.
Minimize Host When Waiting for a Call	Minimizes the host dialog box to the taskbar while waiting for a connection; clear the box to display a status dialog box.
Use Windows Screen Saver When Waiting for a Call	Launches the Windows screen saver when host is waiting for a call.
Launch Host at Startup	Loads the host connection item when you start Windows.
Modem Connection Callback Delay	Specifies how long the host PC waits before calling the remote PC back; this setting is directly affected by the options entered in the Callers tab of the Properties dialog box. See Lesson 10 for more information.

To change the Settings, open the connection item's Properties dialog box and choose the Settings tab. When you're done, choose OK to close the dialog box or click Apply to accept the changes in the tab and choose another tab to modify.

In this lesson, you learned how to create a host connection item and modify the host connection. In the next lesson, you learn to configure host callers.

10

CONFIGURING HOST CALLERS

In this lesson, you'll learn how to create a caller, modify the caller, and set a caller's password.

CREATE A CALLER

When configuring a computer to be a host, you can choose to allow all callers full access, or you can specify caller privileges for individuals. You might want to assign certain callers rights that limit access to the host computer for security reasons. If you let anyone call at any one time, you can't always keep track of their activities.

 Caller The caller is the remote PC that dials and tries to connect with a host PC.

To create a caller and specify privileges for that individual, follow these steps:

1. In the Be a Host PC window, select the connection item for which you will designate a caller.

2. Choose File, Properties; alternatively, right-click the item and choose Properties from the shortcut menu. The connection item's Properties dialog box appears.

3. Choose the Callers tab, as shown in Figure 10.1.

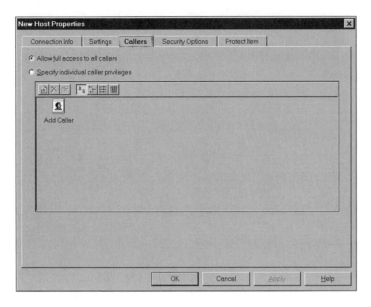

FIGURE 10.1   Configure callers in the Properties dialog box.

4. Choose the Specify Individual Caller Privileges option.

5. Double-click the Add Caller icon; the New Caller Wizard dialog box appears.

6. Enter a name for the caller and click the Next button.

7. Enter the caller's login name and password; confirm the password in the appropriate text box. Click Next.

TIP   **No Password**   You don't have to specify a password; leaving the password text box blank means the caller can log into your computer without any further security. I would, however, recommend you assign passwords to all who call your computer so you can make sure your data is safe and secure.

8. If you want to make any changes before completing the new caller addition, click the Back button to review the previous dialog boxes; otherwise, click the Finish button. The new caller is added to the Callers tab, as shown in Figure 10.2.

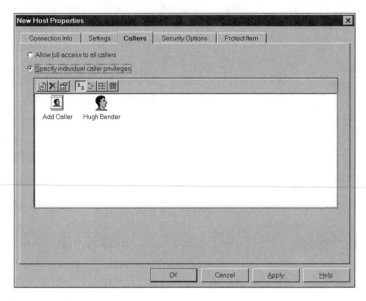

Figure 10.2 Add a new caller so you can specify a password and login name.

You can add more callers, and define security measures for each caller.

Modifying a Caller

After you've added callers to your host PC configuration, you can always modify the settings for a caller. You can delete or rename the caller, change a password or login name, and even copy a caller to a new caller to make creating callers faster.

You make all changes to a caller's settings in the caller's Properties dialog box. To open the dialog box, follow these steps:

1. In the Be a Host PC window, select the connection item for which you will designate a caller.

2. Choose File, Properties; in the Properties dialog box, choose the Callers tab.

3. To modify the caller's properties, right-click the Caller's icon and select Properties from the shortcut menu. The caller's Properties dialog box appears, as shown in Figure 10.3.

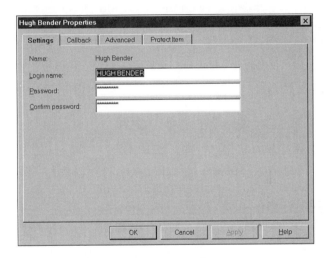

FIGURE 10.3   Set properties for any caller.

Use the directions in the following sections to change options in the Settings, Callback, Advanced, or Protect Item tab.

THE SETTINGS TAB

You can change the original settings for the selected caller by modifying the caller's login name or password.

TIP   **Assign a New Login Name**   To rename a caller, right-click the Caller icon; choose Rename from the shortcut menu and enter the name under the Caller's icon. Press Enter when you're done.

To change the original settings, follow these steps:

1. Click the Settings tab in the Properties dialog box. Enter a new name in the Login Name text box. Press Tab.

2. Enter a new password in the Password text box; you must enter the password again in the Confirm Password text box to confirm the change.

3. Click Apply after changing any option in one of the tabs; this saves the changes so you can modify options in the next tab. Alternatively, click OK to close the dialog box.

The Callback Tab

You set the callback option to protect the host computer. When you set the option, the remote caller dials into the host, and the host notes the call. The remote caller then hangs up, and the server dials the number of the remote caller's modem. Setting this option means more security for your host computer. You can set the remote caller's number ahead of time, offering the most security for the host; or you can let the caller enter the callback number after the connection is made.

To set the callback option, follow these steps:

1. In the Callback tab of the caller's Properties dialog box, check the Call Back the Remote User check box.

2. In the Phone Number text box, enter the number plus area and country code, if applicable. If you leave the text box blank, the remote caller will be prompted to enter a number when she calls the host.

3. Click the Apply button if you want to make other changes in the Properties dialog box; alternatively, choose OK.

THE ADVANCED TAB

The Advanced tab of the caller's Properties dialog box contains multiple caller rights you can set. Alternatively, you can grant the caller full access rights to the host computer.

Setting individual caller's rights gives you the most control over the host PC. To configure Advanced settings, follow these steps:

1. In the Advanced tab of the caller's Properties dialog box, choose options according to Table 10.1. Figure 10.4 shows the Advanced tab options.

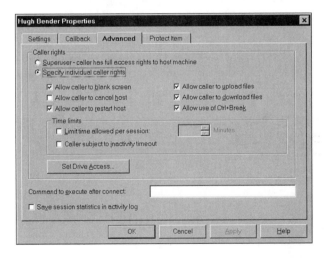

FIGURE 10.4   Use the Advanced tab to further secure the host PC.

Table 10.1   Advanced Caller Options

Option	Description
Caller Rights	
Superuser	Select this option to grant the caller full access to the host computer.
Specify Individual Rights	Select this option to set rights for the individual caller as follows.
Allow Caller to Blank Screen	Enables caller to blank the host PC's screen so no one can see the tasks being performed.
Allow Caller to Cancel Host	Enables remote caller to prohibit other connections.
Allow Caller to Restart Host	Enables caller to reboot or restart the host computer.
Allow Caller to Upload Files	Enables remote caller to send files to the host PC; if you do not check this option, the caller cannot modify the host drive.
Allow Caller to Download Files	Enables the caller to retrieve files from the host PC or perform any operations that modify the drive.
Allow Use of Ctrl+Break	Enables remote caller to use Ctrl+Break to stop certain applications on the host PC.
Time Limits	
Limit Time Allowed Per Session	Check the box and enter a number of minutes to limit the session to; pcANYWHERE will hang up on the caller when the time has expired.

Option	Description
Time Limits	
Caller Subject to Inactivity Timeout	Disconnects if the call is inactive for the specified period; specify the time in the Security Options dialog box of the connection item's Properties dialog box.
Set Drive Access	Select the drives on the host PC to which the remote caller will have access.
Command to Execute After Connect	Enter the path and file name of a program you want to run after the caller logs in.
Save Session Statistics in Activity Log	Records the caller's activities in a log.

2. Choose Apply to save the changes if you want to modify settings in another tab in the dialog box; alternatively, choose OK to close the dialog box.

The Protect Item Tab

You use the Protect Item tab to set a password that sets security for the connection item. If you do not enter a password, any user can access the host PC and view and modify the settings for the caller. If you do enter a password, only those who know the password can view and/or change the caller's properties.

To protect the connection item, follow these steps:

1. In the Protect Item tab of the caller's Properties dialog box, enter a password in the Password text box.

2. Enter the same password in the Confirm Password text box.

3. Choose either or both of the following check boxes to apply to the password:

Required to View Properties   Requires a password for anyone to view the caller's Properties dialog box.

Required to Modify Properties   Requires a password for anyone to change the options in the caller's Properties dialog box.

4. Click Apply to save the changes to the tab and continue to make changes within the Properties dialog box. Alternatively, choose OK to close the dialog box and accept changes.

In this lesson, you learned how to create a caller, modify the caller options, and set a caller's password. In the next lesson, you learn how to set security options.

SETTING SECURITY OPTIONS

In this lesson, you learn how to configure security options and protect the connection item.

CONFIGURING SECURITY OPTIONS

When you enable remote users to access a host PC, you'll want to set certain security options to protect the host PC. Setting options for passwords and login attempts gives you more control over the host and guarantees a shield against callers that don't have permission to connect to the host PC.

Login Attempt A login attempt is when a caller (or remote computer) is unsuccessful at logging into the host PC. A login may be unsuccessful if the user misspelled his or her password, for example, or entered the wrong login name.

You set security options for a host PC's connection item. Table 11.1 describes the options in the Security Options tab of the caller's Properties dialog box.

TABLE 11.1 SECURITY OPTIONS

OPTION	DESCRIPTION
Connection Options Area	
Blank this PC screen after connection made	Makes the host screen blank so that no one near can see what

continues

TABLE 11.1   CONTINUED

OPTION	DESCRIPTION
Connection Options Area	
	the remote caller is doing on-screen.
Log failed connection attempts	Records failed login attempts in a log so you can view them.
Prompt to confirm connection	Prompts the host users to allow the remote connection or not.
Timeout	Enter the number of seconds to wait for the host to confirm the connection.
Disconnect if timeout	If unchecked, the connection is made after timeout expires; if checked, the call is disconnected after the timeout expires.
Login Options Area	
Make passwords case sensitive	Indicates passwords must be entered with the exact uppercase and lowercase characters.
Limit login attempts per call	Enables the user to attempt to log in three times by default if the check box is checked; other wise, you can enter a new number in the Maximum text box.
Limit time to complete login	Indicates the time a remote caller can take to log in; three minutes is the default but you can change the number in the Timeout text box.

OPTION	DESCRIPTION
Session Options	
Data encryption	Enables encryption for the host for all data transferred during session.
Required to access this host	Indicates the host will not accept calls unless the remote caller is using a version of pcANYWHERE that supports data encryption.
Allow any password on reconnect to a session	Enables a remote caller to log in using any password after a session has been unexpectedly disconnected.
Disconnect if inactive	Indicates the connection should be broken if the other end is inactive for a specific period of time; enter the number of minutes to wait in the Timeout text box.

Encryption   The program encrypts, or scrambles, data to prevent hackers from reading the data and or passwords as they transfer across the telephone lines.

To configure the connection item's security options, follow these steps:

1. In the Be A Host PC window, select the connection item you want to configure and choose File, Properties. The host's Properties dialog box appears.

2. Choose the Security Options tab, as shown in Figure 11.1.

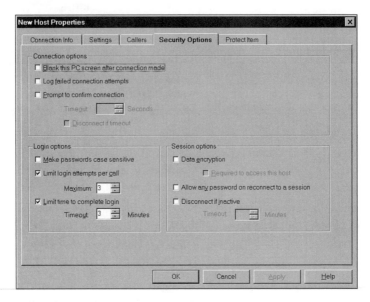

FIGURE 11.1   Set security options to protect the host PC.

3. Choose any of the options described in Table 11.1.

4. Choose Apply to save the changes to the tab and to continue configurations with another tab in the dialog box; alternatively, choose OK to save changes and close the dialog box.

PROTECTING AN ITEM

You can protect a connection item from anyone with access to the host PC who can view, execute, or modify the item. When you don't want others to change the settings you've configured in the host's Properties dialog box, or when you want only those who have the password to be able to make changes, you set a password in the Protect Item tab of the host's Properties dialog box.

To protect a host connection item, follow these steps:

1. In the Be A Host PC window, select the connection item you want to configure and choose File, Properties. The host's Properties dialog box appears.

2. Choose the Protect Item tab.

3. To protect the connection item, enter a password in the Password text box, as shown in Figure 11.2.

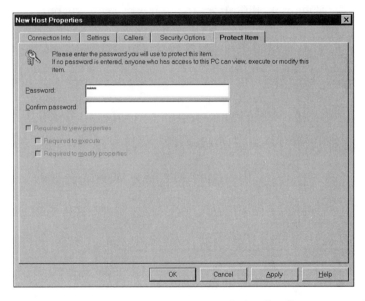

FIGURE 11.2   As you enter the password, the Confirm password text box opens.

4. Enter the password again in the Confirm password text box.

5. Optionally, choose from the following choices:

> Required to view properties   Check this box to call for the password to open the Properties dialog box and view the settings. If you choose this option, the

Required to Modify properties check box is automatically activated and the Required to Execute option becomes available.

Required to execute   Select this option to require the user to enter a password before he can activate the host connection item.

Required to modify properties   Check box to require the user to enter the password before he can make modifications to the Properties dialog box.

6. Choose Apply to save the changes to the tab and to continue configurations with another tab in the dialog box; alternatively, choose OK to save changes and close the dialog box.

In this lesson, you learned how to configure security options and protect the connection item. In the next lesson, you learn to run a host session.

RUNNING A HOST SESSION

In this lesson, you learn how to receive a call, call back a remote caller, print host files from a remote PC, and end a session.

BEGINNING A HOST SESSION

After you configure the host PC, you can begin a host session in any of three ways: launch the host and wait for a call, initiate the call to the remote PC, or call back the remote PC.

Launching the host PC simply makes it ready to receive a call. The host connection item can run in the background while you work on the PC, or you can enable the PC to display a screen saver while waiting for calls.

Use a Screen Saver You set the screen saver option in the Settings tab of the host connection item's Properties dialog box, as described in Lesson 9, "Configuring Host Connections."

Initiating a call to the remote PC enables the host PC to dial and connect to a PC through a specified number. After connection, the remote PC controls the actions of the host PC.

Finally, you can configure the host PC to call the remote PC back. The remote PC first calls the host, the host disconnects from the remote, and then calls it back to initiate the session.

RECEIVING A CALL

When you launch the host PC, it waits for a call that conforms to the configuration of the host connection item's Properties dialog box, as described in Lesson 9, "Configuring Host Connections."

To prepare the host PC to receive a call, follow these steps:

1. Open the Be A Host PC window.

2. Double-click the host connection item; alternatively, right-click the connection item and choose Launch Host from the shortcut menu.

> **Modem to Modem** The host connection must use the
> **TIP** same connection device—modem, for example, or net-
> work, cable, or other device—as the remote PC.

The host connection item remains open, ready for a call from a remote PC. Figure 12.1 shows the waiting host PC connection item; choose Cancel to close the connection at any time.

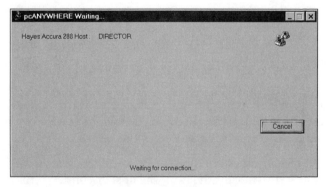

FIGURE 12.1 Launch the host and wait for a call.

INITIATING A CALL

You can call a remote PC from the host to make a connection. After you make the connection, the remote PC controls the activities on the host PC.

To initiate a call from the host, follow these steps:

1. Open the Be A Host PC window.

2. Right-click the host connection item and choose Call Remote from the shortcut menu. The pcANYWHERE Waiting dialog box appears (see Figure 12.2).

3. Enter the phone number and choose OK. The remote PC must be waiting to receive the call, as described in Lesson 13, "Configuring a Remote Control Connection."

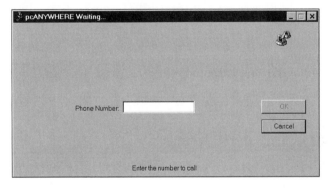

FIGURE 12.2 Enter the phone number of the remote PC.

 No Phone Number Text Box? If the Host PC connection item was configured with a network connection instead of a modem connection, you won't see the dialog box with the Phone Number text box; instead, you'll choose a network host from the Network host list box.

CALLING BACK A REMOTE

If you've configured the host connection item to perform a call-back to connect to a specific remote computer and caller, the process is pretty straightforward. As described in Lesson 10, "Configuring Host Callers," you specify callback settings in the caller's Properties dialog box. Naturally, if you initiate the call, callback is not necessary.

You first launch the host connection to make it available to remote callers. When a caller accesses the host PC, he or she is prompted for a phone number, if you specified this option in the caller's Properties dialog box (see Lesson 10). The host PC then disconnects the caller and initiates a call to the specified phone number.

Info About Sessions For more information about running the session, see Lesson 14, "Running a Remote Control Session." For information about using the pcANYWHERE File Manager, see Lesson 17, "Using the pcANYWHERE File Manager."

RUNNING THE SESSION

When a remote caller calls the host PC, depending on the host PC's configurations, the remote caller may be prompted for a password, a callback number, or other information to complete the connection. After the connection is complete, the remote user has control over the host PC, its files, resources, and so on.

Figure 12.3 shows the session screen that appears upon a successful connection. For more information about running the session and using the pcANYWHERE File Manager, see Lesson 19, "Customizing pcANYWHERE."

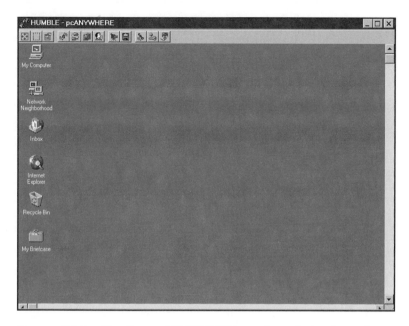

FIGURE 12.3   Use the pcANYWHERE session window to perform tasks in the remote computer.

PRINTING HOST FILES TO THE REMOTE PRINTER

A remote PC can print host files to a local printer (one connected to the remote PC) during a session. However, the host PC must first install the remote printer.

To install a printer to the host PC, follow these steps:

1. Choose Start, Settings, Printers.

2. Double-click the Add Printer icon.

3. The Install New Printer Wizard dialog boxes guide you to installing a new printer.

4. When prompted, be sure to choose Local printer as opposed to network printer.

5. Choose the printer's manufacuturer and model of the printer.

6. When prompted to choose the port for the printer, choose pcaw.prn.

7. Enter a name for the printer when prompted by the Wizard. Choose Finish to complete the installation process.

Ending a Session

When you're finished working with the remote connection, you can end the connection.

 TIP **Do You Use a Phone Center?** If you have a phone center on your PC, you'll have to exit that application (even if it's not currently in use) in order to have access to your modem for pcANYWHERE.

To disconnect, use the taskbar to display the Connected to dialog box. Click the Disconnect button. pcANYWHERE closes the connection.

In this lesson, you learned how to receive a call, call back a remote caller, print from a remote, and end a session. In the next lesson, you learn to configure a remote control connection.

CONFIGURING A REMOTE CONTROL CONNECTION

In this lesson, you learn to create and modify a remote control connection.

UNDERSTANDING A REMOTE CONTROL CONNECTION

Using remote control between computers enables the user of one computer to operate the other computer, remotely. You might want to remotely control another computer if you're working from home and want to transfer some files to your work PC, if you need a file from your work computer and want to print it out at your hotel room on the road, or to troubleshoot a remote PC, for example.

Before creating a remote connection be sure:

- Both computers have pcANYWHERE installed. The remote connection won't work otherwise.

- Both the remote and the host PCs are configured to use the same connection device, a modem or parallel port, for example. If you're just using the remote portion of pcANYWHERE, you don't have to worry about the host portion; someone else must set it up, however.

- Before creating and configuring the remote control connection item, you create, configure, and then launch the host PC connection item as explained in Lessons 9 through 12.

You launch the host PC connection item. The remote PC then calls the host to initiate the session. It is the remote PC that connects to and controls the host PC.

CREATING THE REMOTE CONTROL CONNECTION

You can use the Wizard supplied by pcANYWHERE to create a remote control connection item or you can create the item manually. When you use the Add Remote Control Item Wizard, you assign a name and connection device to the item and the Wizard uses the default settings for the rest of the connection item. You can always customize the default settings in the item's Properties dialog box, as explained later in this lesson.

Default Connection Items   In the Remote Control window, as in other windows of pcANYWHERE, there are default connection items for direct, modem, network, and RAS (Remote Access Service in Windows NT computers) connections. You can use any of these connection items and modify the configurations to suit your purposes, or you can create new items, as explained in this section.

To create a remote control connection item, follow these steps:

1. Click the Remote Control Action button to open the Remote Control window, as shown in Figure 13.1.

2. Double-click the Add Remote Control Item icon to start the Wizard.

Manually Creating an Item   You can manually create an item by selecting File, New and choosing configuration settings from the item's Properties dialog box, explained in the next section.

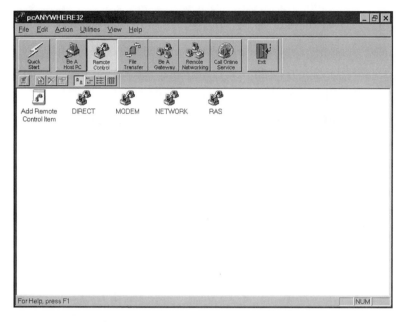

FIGURE 13.1   Open the Remote Control window from the Action bar.

3. In the first Wizard dialog box, enter a name for the connection item and choose Next.

4. In the next Wizard dialog box, choose the connection device in the drop-down list box; click the Details button to further configure the device. Figure 13.2 shows the second Wizard dialog box.

5. Enter the host's phone number and choose Next.

6. In the last Wizard dialog box, check the box to automatically begin the remote session or clear the box to end the creation of the item without connecting at this time. Choose Finish. The item is added to the Remote Control window.

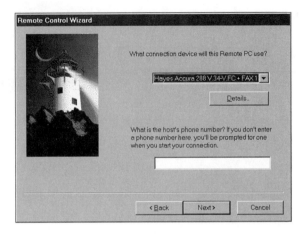

Figure 13.2   Choose a device and configure it, if you want.

MODIFYING A CONNECTION ITEM

You can modify a new or existing connection item to change such settings as the connection device, session settings, password protection, and so on. If you used the Wizard to create an item, there are several default settings you might want to change; or you can change an existing connection item to better suit your circumstances.

CHANGING CONNECTION INFO

The Connection Info tab enables you to change the device and to configure the device, if necessary. For example, you can choose a modem as a device and then configure the modem's speed, parity, and other factors. You can choose up to two devices for any one connection item; for example, choose to a network protocol and a modem so the PC can connect using either.

To modify a connection item, follow these steps:

1. In the Remote Control window, right-click the remote control connection item, and then choose Properties from the shortcut menu.

2. In the remote control PC's Properties dialog box, choose the Connection Info tab to choose up to two devices from the list (see Figure 13.3).

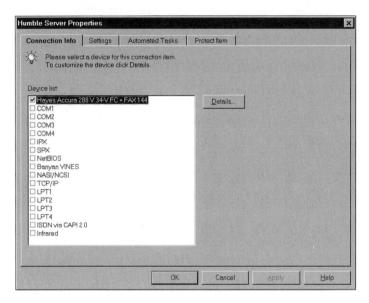

FIGURE 13.3   Choose one or two devices to use to make a remote control connection.

3. Optionally, select a device and click the Details button to configure the device. Choose OK to return to the Properties dialog box.

4. Choose Apply to save the changes to the Connection Info tab and continue to view and modify other tabs in the dialog box; alternatively, choose OK to save the changes and close the dialog box.

TIP   **Rename Item**   To rename a connection item, right-click the item in the Remote Control window and choose Rename from the shortcut menu. Enter the new name and press the Enter key.

CHANGING SETTINGS

The information in the Settings tab of the Properties dialog box are the phone number you entered when you used the Wizard to create the remote control connection item, the number of redial attempts, and the seconds between attempts. You can modify the phone number and other settings for that connection item.

Network Connection If your connection is via network as opposed to a modem connection, you'll need to enter the host name in the Network Host PC to Control text box, located in the Settings tab.

If you're using a TCP/IP connection, you'll need to know the host's DNS name, IP address, or a specific group IP address. Ask your system administrator for this information.

To change Settings, follow these steps:

1. In the Remote Control window, right-click the remote control connection item and choose Properties from the shortcut menu.

2. In the remote control PC's Properties dialog box, choose the Settings tab (see Figure 13.4).

3. Choose the Use Dialing Properties and Phone Number option to enter the number and change dialing properties.

Dialing Properties You use dialing properties to enter such information as calling card numbers, the number to dial for an outside line, and so on.

4. Optionally in Login Information, check the box in front of Automatically Login to Host Upon Connection. Enter

your login name and password for the host computer. Confirm the password in the appropriate text box.

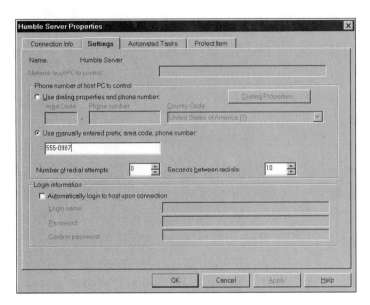

FIGURE 13.4 Enter dialing properties and login information.

 Log in Later You don't have to enter a login name and password at this time, in case you're afraid someone will have access to your personal information. First, the password displays as asterisks, so no one can read it on screen. Second, you can use the Protect Item tab to set security on the item, as explained in the next section. Finally, you can wait until you connect to the host PC, at which time you'll be prompted for your login name and password.

5. Choose Apply to save the changes to the Connection Info tab and continue to view and modify other tabs in the dialog box; alternatively, choose OK to save the changes and close the dialog box.

PROTECTING AN ITEM

You use the Protect Item tab to set a password that sets security for the connection item. If you enter a password, only those who know the password can view and/or change the item's properties.

To protect the connection item, follow these steps:

1. In the Protect Item tab of the remote control connection item's Properties dialog box, enter a password in the Password text box.

2. Enter the same password in the Confirm Password text box.

3. Choose either or both of the following check boxes to apply to the password:

   Required to View Properties   Requires a password for anyone to view the item's Properties dialog box.

   Required to Modify Properties   Requires a password for anyone to change the options in the item's Properties dialog box.

4. Click Apply to save the changes to the tab and continue to make changes within the Properties dialog box. Alternatively, choose OK to close the dialog box and accept changes.

 TIP **Automated Tasks**   To find out how to configure the Automated Tasks tab of the item's Properties dialog box, see Lesson 15.

In this lesson, you learned to create and modify a remote control connection. In the next lesson, you learn to run a remote control session.

RUNNING THE REMOTE CONTROL SESSION

In this lesson, you learn how to start the remote control session, perform tasks on the remote computer, and end the session.

STARTING THE SESSION VIA MODEM

Whether you're using a network connection or a modem connection for a remote control session, the procedures for beginning the session are similar. After you configure the connection items, the remote PC attaches to the host PC and can then control the host.

> **TIP** **Host Initiated Session** As described in Lesson 12, a remote control session may also be initiated by a host PC.
>
> When you're expecting a call from a host, you'll need to prepare the remote PC for that call. Right-click the Remote Control Connection item and choose Wait for Connection from the shortcut menu. When the connection is made, the host's screen appears in a session window on the remote.

To start the remote control session by calling the host PC, follow these steps:

1. Choose the Remote Control Action button to display the Remote Control window.

2. Double-click the connection item that uses the same device as the host PC you plan to call; alternatively, you can right-click the connection item and choose Connect from the shortcut menu.

3. Depending on the configuration, you may be prompted for a login name and password to gain access to the host PC. Next, the host's screen appears in a remote session window, as shown in Figure 14.1. See Lesson 19 for information about performing tasks in the remote session window.

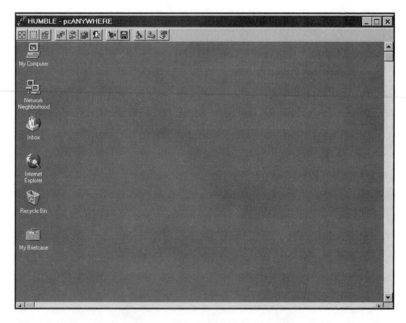

Figure 14.1   When you see the remote session window with the host's screen in it, you can begin the session.

 TIP   **Remote PCs**   A remote PC may also be configured to automatically start a file transfer; see Lessons 16 and 17 for more information.

STARTING A SESSION OVER THE NETWORK

You can make a network connection to a host using pcANYWHERE. The network connection uses a network protocol to make the connection, such as NetBEUI or TCP/IP (see Appendix B for more about connection types). You set the protocol as the device in the Connection Info tab of the item's Properties dialog box.

Protocol   A protocol is a set of procedures networking and communications transmit and receive data.

NetBEUI   (NetBIOS Extended User Interface) A protocol used to communicate between two computers; often used with Microsoft networks.

TCP/IP   (Transmission Control Protocol/Internet Protocol) A set of communications protocols popular with a large number of hardware and software vendors, available on many different types of computers, and is used as the basis of the Internet.

When you use a network connection, you'll also need to enter a Network Host PC name in the Settings tab of the Properties dialog box. If you neglect to enter a host's name, you're prompted to choose the host when you connect to the network using pcANYWHERE.

Using NetBEUI or another protocol is pretty straightforward because there are few settings to configure; just choose the protocol and make the call.

Using TCP/IP is a bit more difficult. You can configure TCP/IP to connect to one or multiple hosts on the network by using a DNS (Domain Name Service) in the Network Host PC to Control box,

Settings tab. The DNS name is assigned by your network administrator. If you're not familiar with configuring TCP/IP, see your network administrator.

If you plan to connect to a host PC through an Internet service provider, you can enter a specific group IP address, such as **120.45.62**, and then enter **255** as the last number in the address to force pcANYWHERE to list all hosts on the subnet with IP addresses beginning with **120.45.62**. You can then choose from the hosts that list before the connection.

If you've listed TCP/IP hosts in the Application Options dialog box (as described in Lesson 19), those host names and addresses are used unless you enter a host name in the Network Host PC to Control text box of the Settings tab in the Properties dialog box.

To connect using a network connection, follow these steps:

1. In the Remote Control window, right-click the connection item's icon and choose Properties from the shortcut menu.

2. In the Connection Info tab, make sure you've selected the appropriate protocol as the device type. Choose OK.

3. Double-click the connection item's icon. pcANYWHERE searches for the host computer(s) and displays the pcANYWHERE Waiting dialog box as shown in Figure 14.2.

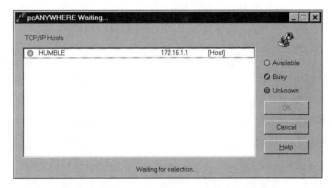

Figure 14.2   Choose the available host to connect to.

4. Select an available host—one with a green dot in front of it—and choose OK.

After connection, the host's screen is displayed in a session window, just as with a modem connection (refer to Figure 14.1). See Lesson 19 for information about using the session window.

CONNECTING TO MULTIPLE HOSTS

When you connect to multiple hosts, you're actually starting up multiple pcANYWHERE applications within Windows. You can call one host, minimize pcANYWHERE, and then open another pcANYWHERE program window and connect to the second host.

You must first tell pcANYWHERE to allow connection to multiple hosts, as follows:

1. Choose File, Application Options and select the Remote Operation tab.

2. Choose the Allow Connection to Multiple Hosts check box and then click Apply to save the changes.

3. Click OK to close the dialog box and save the changes.

To connect to multiple hosts, follow these steps:

1. In the open pcANYWHERE program, connect to the first host.

2. Minimize pcANYWHERE and choose Start, Programs, pcANYWHERE, pcANYWHERE to start a second pcANYWHERE program.

3. Connect to the second host. Click the icon on the taskbar to switch back and forth between the two open sessions.

Ending the Session

You can end the session by clicking the Close button in the title bar of the session window; alternatively, right-click the icon in the taskbar and choose Close. A confirmation dialog box appears; choose Yes to end the session.

In this lesson, you learned how to start the remote control session, perform tasks on the remote computer, and end the session. In the next lesson, you learn how to configure automated tasks.

CONFIGURING AUTOMATED TASKS

In this lesson, you learn how to create and configure an automated task.

CREATING AN AUTOMATED TASK

When using remote control on a host computer, you can use pcANYWHERE's automated tasks to perform chores for you automatically upon connection. You might, for example, want to run a file that sets certain configurations on the host; or you could transfer multiple files upon connection, automatically, using AutoXfer, or automatic transfer.

AutoXfer An AutoXfer procedure is a file that contains commands to automatically transfer files from one computer to the other, or to synchronize files between the two computers.

Synchronize Copying only the files with the latest time stamps on them so as to ensure all files on the host and the remote PC are up-to-date.

TIP

More on AutoXfer For more information about AutoXfer, see Lesson 16.

To configure an automated task, follow these steps:

1. In the Remote Control window, right-click the connection item and choose Properties from the shortcut menu.

2. In the item's Properties dialog box, choose the Automated Tasks tab, as shown in Figure 15.1.

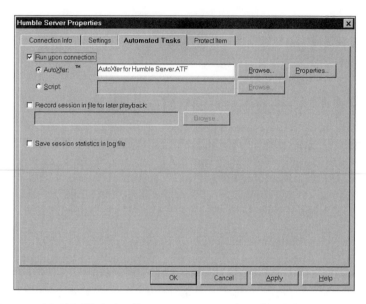

Figure 15.1   Click the Run upon connection check box to display the rest of the options on the tab.

3. Click the Run upon connection check box; this option causes the execution of a file when the session begins.

4. Choose either the AutoXfer or the Script option. AutoXfer, or automatic transfer, automatically performs a file transfer when you choose this option.

Script A script file is a small program that executes some specific set of instructions each time the user logs in to a computer, for example, or that sends the user identification to the PC. For more about creating scripts, see the manual that comes with your pcANYWHERE software.

5. Optionally, check the Record Session in File for Later Playback check box to record activities to a file. Enter a file name in the text box or use the Browse button to specify an existing file to tÛ% for the log.

6. Optionally, check the Save Session Statistics in Log File check box to record statistics about the session; you'll be prompted for a file name for this log after the session is disconnected.

MODIFYING AN AUTOXFER PROCEDURE

After setting the AutoXfer procedure to run on connection, you can add file transfer commands to the procedure. When you configure the transfer commands, you also list the files you want to transfer, either to the host or to the remote PC.

You can modify the contents of the procedure, commands and files, and the options that define the procedure.

MODIFYING THE CONTENTS

When you modify the contents of the file transfer procedure, you're selecting the files, folders, subfolders, and files, and so on that you want to transfer automatically.

To modify the AutoXfer procedure, follow these steps:

1. In the item's Properties dialog box, Automated Tasks tab, choose the AutoXfer option and then select Properties. The Properties dialog box appears, as shown in Figure 15.2.

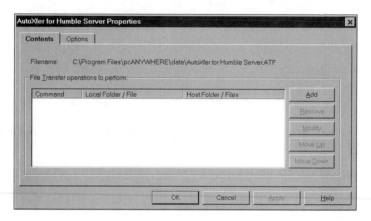

Figure 15.2   Modify the AutoXfer properties.

2. In the Contents tab, choose the Add button to add commands to the procedure. The Add AutoXfer Command dialog box appears (see Figure 15.3).

Figure 15.3   Add commands to the AutoXfer procedure.

3. In the Select Type of Transfer area, choose one of the following:

> Send to host   Choose this option to send a file or folder from the remote PC to the host PC.

> Receive from host   Choose this option to receive a file or folder from the host PC to the remote PC.

> Sync   Choose this option to synchronize one or more files between the host and the remote PCs. Synchronizing files means only the most up-to-date files are saved on both computers.

4. In the Specify folder/file for transfer text box, enter the file or folder name that will be transferred.

 TIP   **Subfolders Not Included**   Since subfolders of a folder are not included in an AutoXfer command, you must create a command for each subfolder you want to transfer.

---

5. Choose OK to close the Add AutoXfer Command dialog box.

6. In the Contents tab, you can make any of the following additional changes:

- Use the Add button in the Contents tab to list additional commands, files, or folders to transfer.

- Use the Remove button to remove a selected command from the File Transfer Operations to Perform list.

- Click the Modify button to change file names or other information about the selected command.

- Click Move Up or Move Down to adjust the position of the selected command in the File Transfer Operations to Perform list.

7. Commands are carried out according to their order in the list. Click Apply to put options into effect and click the Options tab to change more options (see the next section), or click OK to save changes and exit the Properties dialog box.

SETTING OPTIONS

Use the options in the Options tab of the item's Properties dialog box to set file transfer configuration or to use the default settings. Some of the options you can choose to keep or override include file compression, crash recovery, and virus checking.

File Compression A technique that shrinks files so they occupy less disk space and take less time to transfer.

Crash Recovery A technique that salvages a session if one computer or the other crashes, or shuts off for some reason, during the file transfer.

Virus Checking A program that checks files for viruses before writing them to disk so a virus isn't transferred to the host computer.

To set options, follow these steps:

1. In the item's Properties dialog box, Automated Tasks tab, choose the AutoXfer option and then select Properties. The Properties dialog box appears.

2. Choose the Options tab.

3. If you want to change the default options, select Override file transfer options for this Automated Transfer, as shown in Figure 15.4.

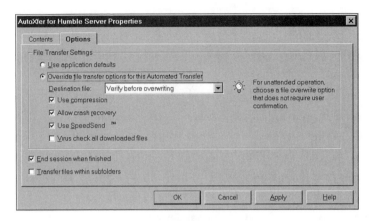

FIGURE 15.4   Change the file transfer options.

4. In Destination file, choose the option from the list box; you can choose to never or always overwrite files of the same name, to verify before overwriting, to overwrite older files only, or to always prompt for a destination.

5. Optionally, choose from the following check boxes:

> **Use compression**   Checked, this option compresses files for transfer.

> **Allow crash recovery**   Checked, this option enables the program to recover in case one or the other of the computers crashes during the transfer, so all data is not lost.

> **Use SpeedSend**   Checked, this option speeds the transfer of files.

> **Virus check all downloaded files**   Checked, this option scans files for viruses.

Quicker transfer   If you do not check the Virus Check option, your file transfer is quicker; but be careful, you may also get a virus from the transferred files.

6. Optionally, check the End session when finished to disconnect as soon as the commands are carried out and the transfer is complete.

7. Optionally, check Transfer files within subfolders to get the files as well as the subfolders.

8. Choose OK to save the changes and close the dialog box.

In this lesson, you learned how to create an automated task and to create and configure an AutoXfer procedure. In the next lesson, you learn to manage a connection session.

Using the pcANYWHERE Session Window

In this lesson, you learn to use the pcANYWHERE session window to perform tasks during a remote session.

Understanding the Session Window

When you successfully connect to a host PC using pcANYWHERE, the host computer's screen appears on your screen in a session window. The pcANYWHERE session window includes several tool buttons you can use to control the session as well as a Control menu that contains special pcANYWHERE commands you can use to control the session.

Remote PC Remote PC or computer refers to the computer on which you are performing these tasks. You are remotely controlling another computer—the host computer. For you to be able to control another computer, the other computer must be in host mode.

Online Menus Access Both the host PC and the remote PC have access to pcANYWHERE's online menus; however, since the remote PC is the one controlling the session, its menus contain more options than the host's.

Figure 16.1 shows the pcANYWHERE menu, which branches from the Control menu in the session window. Table 16.1 describes each command on the pcANYWHERE menu.

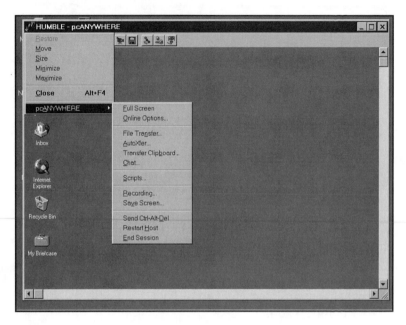

FIGURE 16.1   Use the pcANYWHERE menu to maneuver the session.

TABLE 16.1   pcANYWHERE SESSION WINDOW MENU

COMMAND	DESCRIPTION
Full Screen	Makes the host PC's screen maximized as if it were your screen; press Alt+Enter to return the screen to a session window then choose Execute Locally from the resulting dialog box.
Online Options	Displays the Online Options dialog box in which you can choose settings to apply to the host PC.

COMMAND	DESCRIPTION
File Transfer	Displays the pcANYWHERE File Manager in which you can manipulate files between the two computers.
AutoXfer	Displays the Run AutoXfer dialog box in which you activate the AutoXfer procedure you've previously defined.
Transfer Clipboard	Displays the Transfer Clipboard in which you choose the direction and items you want to transfer; you can transfer the host's Clipboard contents, for instance, to your PC.
Chat	Displays the pcANYWHERE Chat window through which you can communicate with someone on the host PC.
Scripts	Displays the Scripts dialog box in which you create, edit, and run scripts on the host PC.
Save Screen	Displays the Select Save Screen File in which you enter a name and location for saving the screen file.
Restart Host	Reboots the host PC.
End Session	Disconnects from the host computer and ends the session.

Host's Online Menu   The host's online menu contains the following commands: End Session, File Transfer, Chat, Help.

In addition to the menu commands, you can use the tool buttons in the session window to perform several tasks. Table 16.2

describes each of the tool buttons. The buttons correspond to
menu commands as described in Table 16.1.

TABLE 16.2 SESSION WINDOW TOOL BUTTONS

TOOL BUTTON	DESCRIPTION
	Full Screen
	Screen Scaling
	Online Options
	File Transfer
	AutoXfer
	Transfer Clipboard
	Chat
	Recording
	Save Screen
	Ctrl+Alt+Del
	Restart Host
	End Session

CHATTING WITH THE REMOTE PC

When you connect to a host PC, you may find you need to ask the user of that PC a question or ask him or her to perform some task for you to continue your session. You can chat with the user of the host PC via pcANYWHERE.

Either the host or the remote PC can begin a chat session using the Control Menu of the session window and the Chat command. During the chat, one user enters a message and the other user can read that message on-screen and then answer it.

To use the chat utility, follow these steps:

1. Choose the Control menu and then select the pcANYWHERE menu. Choose the Chat command. The pcANYWHERE Chat window displays.

2. Enter the text in the lower (white) pane of the window and press Enter to send the message. When the message is sent, it appears in the upper pane of the window (see Figure 16.2).

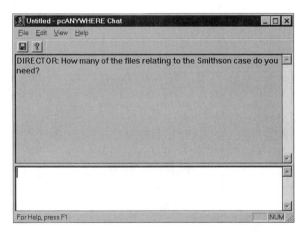

FIGURE 16.2   Enter a message to the remote computer.

3. When you receive an answer from the remote PC, continue the conversation by entering another message in
the lower pane of the window.

4. To exit the Chat utility, choose File, Exit Chat.

> **Save the Chat** If you want to save the contents of the
> **TIP** upper chat window pane, choose File, Save As and
> enter a location and file name. Click Save.

USING AUTOXFER

As discussed in Lesson 15, you can create AutoXfer procedures
that enable you to automatically transfer files between the remote
and host PCs; you also can set synchronization between the two
computers.

You can create an AutoXfer procedure that automatically runs
when the connection is made, as explained in the last lesson. You
can also create, modify, and run an AutoXfer procedure during a
session.

After the session begins, you can run an AutoXfer procedure from
the online menu, by following these steps:

1. Choose the Control menu in the session window. Choose
pcANYWHERE, AutoXfer. The Run AutoXfer dialog box
appears, as shown in Figure 16.3.

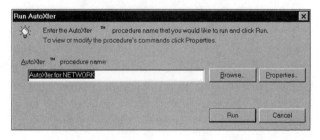

FIGURE 16.3   Create and run an AutoXfer during a session.

2. You can accept the default name or enter a new name; alternatively, choose the Browse button to locate an existing file name.

3. Click the Properties button to display the AutoXfer Properties dialog box. Add, modify, remove, or reorganize the commands and file transfers and then choose OK to close the dialog box. For more information about the AutoXfer Properties dialog box, see Lesson 15.

4. In the Run AutoXfer dialog box, choose Run. pcANYWHERE runs the commands and automatically transfers the files requested.

SETTING ONLINE OPTIONS

The online options include a few settings that could make your session more comfortable and useful. You can choose to scale the host screen to better fit the window, display or hide the remote control toolbar, reduce the number of colors the host uses, and to lock the host's keyboard and blank the host's screen during the session. You might want to lock the keyboard and blank the host's screen so no one can interrupt your session or see what you're doing on the host PC.

Current Session Only   Any changes you make to the Online Options dialog box affect the current session only.

To set the online options, follow these steps:

1. Choose the Control menu from the session window. Choose pcANYWHERE, Online Options. The Online Options dialog box appears (see Figure 16.4).

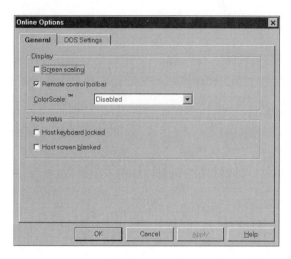

FIGURE 16.4   Set Online Options for the current session.

2. Choose the General tab and check any of the options, as described previously, that you want to activate.

3. Choose OK to accept the changes and close the dialog box.

In this lesson, you learned to use the pcANYWHERE session window to perform tasks during a remote session. In the next lesson, you learn to use the pcANYWHERE File Manager.

USING THE pcANYWHERE FILE MANAGER

In this lesson, you learn to use the pcANYWHERE File Manager to transfer files between the connected computers.

ACCESSING THE FILE MANAGER

You can use the pcANYWHERE File Manager to transfer files between computers and to manage files on both the host and remote PC. You also can access the File Manager on the remote PC or the host PC after the connection between the two is successful.

ACCESSING THE REMOTE FILE MANAGER

The use of the terms *remote* and *host* can be confusing. To clarify, you're running the remote control PC and connecting to a host PC; it is the host PC you will access and control. The remote File Manager, then, is located on your PC.

To open the remote File Manager after successfully connecting to the host, follow these steps:

1. In the session window, choose the Control menu and select pcANYWHERE; alternatively, click the File Transfer icon.

2. From the pcANYWHERE menu, choose File Transfer. The File Manager appears, as shown in Figure 17.1.

Double-click to
view the parent   Computer's   Click here to   Double-click to
directory.   names Select a drive. reverse the   open a folder.
                                           transfer direction.

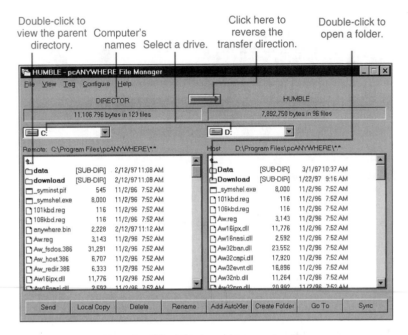

FIGURE 17.1   Use the File Manager to transfer files.

Which Is Which?   The computer on the left is the one from which you are working—the remote control PC. The computer on the right is the host PC.

Parent Directory   In the hierarchical directory system, the parent is the directory immediately above the current directory. The symbol .. (sometimes represented with an arrow and two dots) is shorthand for the name of the parent directory.

ACCESSING THE HOST'S FILE MANAGER

You can access the File Manager from the host PC so you can initiate a file transfer, just as you can with the remote control PC.

To access the File Manager from the host PC after successfully connecting the two computers, follow these steps:

1. Choose Control menu, pcANYWHERE, File Transfer; alternatively, click the File Transfer icon.

2. Then select the Controlled by Host from the submenu. The host's File Manager appears with the host and remote PC's files listed.

EXITING THE FILE MANAGER

To exit the File Manager, either from the host or the remote control PC, choose File, Exit File Manager. pcANYWHERE returns to the session window.

SETTING FILE MANAGER OPTIONS

You can set options in the File Manager that make it easier for you to find files and folders before transferring them. You can sort files and look at file details.

You can change the options in the File Manager as follows:

- To change how the files are sorted in the window, choose the View menu and then select one of the following: By Name, By Ext, By Date, or By Size. The files are listed in the method you specify.

- Choose View, Filter to display only certain files, such as program files, document files, or others for which you are searching.

- To view or hide file details, choose the View menu and choose: Show Date, Show Time, or Show Size. A check mark beside the options indicates it is active; clicking the option again deactivates it and therefore hides that file detail.

SELECTING FILES AND FOLDERS

Before you can transfer files and/or folders, you must select them. Selecting files and folders in the pcANYWHERE File Manager is the same as selecting them in other Windows applications:

 TIP **Indicate the Window in Which You Are Working** To indicate which window you're working in—when selecting files, deleting or renaming files, and so on—click the mouse in that window before performing any tasks.

- To select a file and/or folder, click it so it is highlighted.

- To select multiple contiguous folders or files, click the first file, press and hold the Shift key, and click the last file you want to select. All files between the two become highlighted.

- To select multiple non-contiguous folders or files, click the first file, press and hold the Ctrl key, and click any other files you want to select.

- To deselect one file or folder in a group of selected files, press and hold the Ctrl key, and click the file you want to deselect.

- To deselect all files and folders, click anywhere in the window.

You can also use the Tag menu in the pcANYWHERE File Manager to select files. First, click the window in which you're working. Then, choose Tag and one of the following:

Tag All   Tags, or selects, all files and folders in the window.

Tag Files   Selects only the files in the window, no folders.

Tag Folders   Selects the folders and the files they contain within the active window.

Clear Tags   Clears all selections.

Reverse Tags   Deselects the selected files and folders and selects those files and folders that were previously unselected.

Tag By   Enables you to provide a filter for file or folder selection; for example, type *.doc in the Select Some dialog box and only files ending with the doc extension are tagged.

OTHER FILE MANAGEMENT TECHNIQUES

You can delete files and folders, rename files and folders, and create folders in both the host PC and the remote control PC. The buttons at the bottom of the File Manager provide you with the resources for managing files and folders in the File Manager.

To rename a file or folder, select the file or folder and click the Rename button. The Rename dialog box appears as shown in Figure 17.2. Enter the name in the To text box and choose OK.

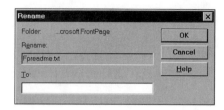

FIGURE 17.2   Rename files and folders on the host or the remote PC.

To delete a file or folder, select it and then click the Delete button. The Delete confirmation dialog box appears. Choose OK to delete the selected file(s) or folder(s).

To go to a folder without searching for it through the list of files and folders, click the Go To button. The Change Folder dialog box appears. Enter the name of the folder in the New Folder text box and choose OK. The File Manager opens that folder in the selected window.

To create a folder, select the window—either host or remote PC—and then select the folder that will serve as the parent to the new folder. Click the Create Folder button. The Create Folder dialog box appears (see Figure 17.3). Enter the name of the new folder to create. Choose OK.

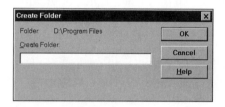

FIGURE 17.3   Create a folder to hold the transferred files, for example.

In this lesson, you learned to use the pcANYWHERE File Manager to transfer files between the connected computers. In the next lesson, you learn to create folders, delete folders, and copy files and folders using the File Manager.

SENDING AND RECEIVING FILES WITH THE FILE MANAGER

In this lesson, you learn how to send files, copy files and folders, and synchronize files and folders.

SENDING AND RECEIVING FILES

You can send files from the remote to the host and receive files from the host to the remote control PC using File Manager. With File Manager, it's easy to select the files and folders to transfer and then indicate the direction of the transfer.

You can start the file transfer from either the host or the remote control PC. Open the File Manager by choosing the Control menu and selecting pcANYWHERE, File Transfer.

TRANSFERRING FILES FROM THE REMOTE

You can transfer files to the host from the remote using the File Manager in pcANYWHERE. For information on selecting files and folders to transfer, see Lesson 17.

To transfer files from the remote to the host PC, follow these steps:

1. On the remote control PC, open the File Manager, and open the drive and folder to which you want to copy the files on the host.

2. Select the files from the remote PC window that you want to send to the host.

3. Click Send; alternatively, you can click the Send button on the File Manager's button bar. The Begin File Transfer dialog box appears (see Figure 18.1).

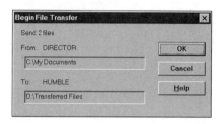

FIGURE 18.1   The To: box lists the open folder on the host that will receive the transferred files.

4. Choose OK to transfer the files from the remote PC to the host PC. A File Transfer Status dialog box appears to show you the progress and the final statistics of the transfer (see Figure 18.2).

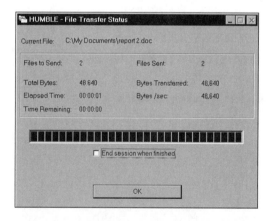

FIGURE 18.2   The File Transfer Status dialog box shows you the statistics of the transfer.

5. Click OK to close the dialog box; you can click the End Session When Finished check box to close the session when the transfer is complete.

No File Transfer Status Dialog Box? If you do not see the File Transfer Status dialog box, it may be minimized during the session. See Lesson 19 for information about customizing pcANYWHERE.

TRANSFERRING FILES FROM THE HOST

You can transfer files from the host using File Manager on the remote control PC; simply select the files you want in the host side of the window and click the red direction indicator arrow to change the direction of the transfer.

You can also transfer files from the host PC if you are running the host instead of the remote control PC. The process is very similar. Follow these steps:

1. On the host PC, choose Control menu, and select pcANYWHERE, File Transfer, Controlled by Host. The File Manager on the host appears.

2. From File Manager, select the files and folders to transfer and click Send.

3. The File Transfer Status dialog box is displayed on the remote control PC. When the transfer is complete on the remote control PC, click OK.

SETTING FILE TRANSFER OPTIONS

Just as with your AutoXfer procedures, you can set file transfer options that affect any files you select and transfer during a session. Those options control overwriting files, file compression, and crash recovery. You can make the changes to these options at any time while online with the host computer.

To set file transfer options, follow these steps:

1. In File Manager, choose Configure, File Transfer Options. The File Transfer Options dialog box appears, as shown in Figure 18.3.

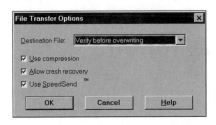

Figure 18.3   Set options for the file transfer.

2. Choose the overwrite setting from the Destination File drop-down list; you can choose to never overwrite duplicate files, always overwrite duplicate files, verify before overwriting, always ask for destination, or overwrite older files only.

3. Check one or more of the following to activate the option, or clear the check from the option's box to deactivate the option:

   Use compression   Compresses the files during transfer so the transfer is faster. Decompresses the files after they arrive at the destination.

   Allow Crash Recovery   Sets the option so that if there is a crash of the host or remote PC during the transfer, all transferred files are not lost.

   Use SpeedSend   Enables quicker transferring of files.

4. Choose OK to return to File Manager.

COPYING FILES AND FOLDERS

You can create a local copy of a file or folder on the host or on the remote PC. When you're copying files using the Local Copy command, however, you're not copying files from one computer to another; you're just making an additional copy of the file on the same computer that contains the original.You might want to copy a file in this manner if that file is also accessed by other users. Because pcANYWHERE needs the file exclusively in order to transfer, you can copy it (which takes only a minute or two) rather than transfer it directly (which may take an hour or so). That way, other users won't be delayed so long in their use of the file.

You'll need to give the new copy of the file a new name or a location other than the folder containing the original.

To copy files and folders, follow these steps:

1. In the File Manager, select the file or folder you want to copy.

2. Choose File, Local Copy. The Copy dialog box appears (see Figure 18.4).

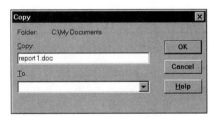

FIGURE 18.4   Make a local copy of a file or folder.

3. Enter the name or location of the copy. Choose OK.

Synchronizing Files and Folders

You synchronize files and folders to make sure that the files on the host and remote PCs are identical to each other. Synchronization changes the folders on both the host and remote PC by copying the files from one to the other so the contents of the folder are exactly the same. Therefore, if a file exists in the folder on the remote but doesn't exist in the folder on the host, pcANYWHERE copies that file to the host, and vice versa. Additionally, when duplicate file names appear, the file with the most current date is copied.

TIP **Cloning?** Cloning is similar to synchronizing except that when you clone a folder, pcANYWHERE deletes any files in the destination folder that do not exist in the source folder. Synchronization doesn't delete any files.

Comparing Files and Folders

Before you synchronize folders and files, you should compare them first. pcANYWHERE's Compare utility searches both the host and remote folders and tells you if they are the same or different. Comparing also lists the different and missing files, but takes no action between the two folders.

To compare two folders, follow these steps:

1. In File Manager, open the folders to be compared on the host and the remote PCs.

2. Choose File, Compare Folders. If the files are different, pcANYWHERE displays a warning dialog box telling you the files are different and then highlights the files. If the files are the same, pcANYWHERE notifies you of that fact as well.

SYNCHRONIZING

Synchronizing folders is an excellent method of assuring that the files on both the host and the remote PCs are updated.

To synchronize files and folders, follow these steps:

1. In the File Manager, select the folders you want to synchronize.

2. Choose File, Synchronize; alternatively, click the Sync button in File Manager. pcANYWHERE displays the Synchronize Folder dialog box, as shown in Figure 18.5.

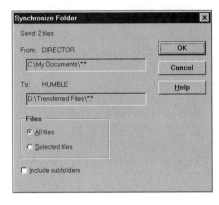

FIGURE 18.5   Synchronize folders and files between two computers.

3. Verify that the correct folders are selected and then choose OK. pcANYWHERE displays the File Transfer Status dialog box to show the statistics of the transfer.

4. Click OK to close the File Transfer Status dialog box and return to the pcANYWHERE File Manager.

Synchronizing Files Only   If you want to synchronize selected files from a folder, open File Manager and then open the folders on the host and remote that contain the files to be synchronized. Choose View, Filter and choose the file type you want to synchronize. Choose OK and then continue with your synchronization.

In this lesson, you learned how to send files, copy files and folders, and synchronize files and folders. In the next lesson, you learn to customize pcANYWHERE.

Customizing pcANYWHERE

In this lesson, you learn to change your computer's name, set dialing properties, and customize file transfer.

Changing System Setup

System setup includes two items you can change to customize pcANYWHERE: your computer's name and the dialing properties for your computer.

By default, your computer uses the name you entered during the Windows setup; you can change the name that pcANYWHERE will use to identify you to other computers.

Dialing properties define your location, area code, country code, and other information pcANYWHERE uses to dial remote computers.

Changing the Computer's Name

You can change your computer's name, which is how your computer is identified to any host PC or remote PC that connects via pcANYWHERE. You can use the same name as you entered during Windows 95 or Windows NT setup, or you can change that name.

To change the computer's name that pcANYWHERE uses, follow these steps:

1. Choose File, Application Options. The Application Options dialog box appears, as shown in Figure 19.1.

FIGURE 19.1 Change your computer's name in the System Setup tab of the Application Options dialog box.

2. In the System Setup tab, choose the User Defined option in Your Computer Name Selection.

3. Enter the name by which you want your computer to be identified.

4. Choose Apply to save the changes to the tab and leave the dialog box open to modify other settings. Or, choose OK to save the settings you've changed and close the dialog box.

SETTING UP DIALING PROPERTIES

You can customize the dialing properties pcANYWHERE uses to connect to other computers via modem. For example, you can enter a calling card number or disable call waiting.

To set up dialing properties, follow these steps:

1. In the Application options dialog box, System Setup tab (refer to Figure 19.1), choose the Dialing Properties button. The Dialing Properties dialog box appears.

2. To create a new location, say one you might use from home or on the road with your computer, choose the New button and enter the new location name in the Create New Location dialog box. Choose OK to return to the Dialing Properties dialog box.

3. Enter the area and country codes for the location from which you are dialing.

4. Optionally, enter a number to dial for accessing an outside or long distance line in the How Do I Dial From This Location? area.

5. If you want to use a calling card to charge the call, check the Dial Using Calling Card option and choose Change to enter the card number.

6. To disable call waiting, check the box in front of the This Location Has Call Waiting option and enter the number in the text box provided.

7. Choose whether the phone system uses tone or pulse dialing.

8. Choose OK to close the Dialing Properties dialog box and return to the Application Options dialog box.

9. Choose Apply to save the changes to the tab and leave the dialog box open to modify other settings. Or choose OK to save the settings you've changed and close the dialog box.

Customizing Remote Operations

You can modify the way pcANYWHERE handles remote control sessions. If you change these options during a session, the changes only apply to the current session; however, if you change the options when you're not in the middle of a session, the changes affect all sessions.

To customize remote operations for all sessions, follow these steps:

1. Choose File, Application Options. The Application Options dialog box appears.

2. Choose the Remote Operation tab, as shown in Figure 19.2.

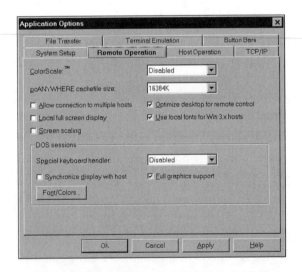

Figure 19.2 Modify settings for remote control sessions.

3. Make any changes in the options as described in Table 19.1.

4. Choose Apply to save the changes to the tab and leave the dialog box open to modify other settings. Or, choose OK to save the settings you've changed and close the dialog box.

TABLE **19.1** REMOTE OPERATION OPTIONS

OPTION	DESCRIPTION
ColorScale	Indicates the number of colors for translated bitmaps; choosing two or four colors optimizes the screen display on the remote control PC.
Cachefile Size	Indicates the size of the cache during a remote control session.
Allow Connection to Multiple Hosts	Check this option to enable connection to more than one host by starting more than one pcANYWHERE application at a time.
Local Full Screen Display	Checked, automatically displays the host screen full-screen on the remote; unchecked, displays the host screen in a window.
Screen Scaling	Scales the host screen to fit in the remote's terminal window, as opposed to making the remote scroll the window to see everything on-screen.
Optimize Desktop for Remote Control	Disables any desktop wallpaper patterns, screen savers, and so on, on the host PC to improve performance over the connection.
Use Local Fonts for Win 3.x Hosts	Forces the remote PC to use a local font that matches the font of the Windows 3.x host to improve performance.

Cachefile Size   The cache is an area of memory that improves performance by storing the contents of frequently accessed files or other objects. In pcANYWHERE, the cache stores bitmap information during the remote session so that data doesn't have to be sent each time the Windows screen is redrawn. The cachefile size refers to the amount of disk space set aside for the cache.

TIP

Speed Up Operations   If you choose to disable the ColorScale option, you can improve performance during the transfer.

If you plan to run the host using a DOS screen, use the options in the DOS Sessions area of the Remote Operation tab.

SETTING FILE TRANSFER OPTIONS

The file transfer options you set indicate the download folder to which all files automatically download and the protocol used to transfer files.

To set file transfer options, follow these steps:

1. Choose File, Application Options. The Application Options dialog box appears.

2. Choose the File Transfer tab, as shown in Figure 19.3.

3. Choose options as described in Table 19.2.

4. Choose Apply to save the changes to the tab and leave the dialog box open to modify other settings. Or, choose OK to save the settings you've changed and close the dialog box.

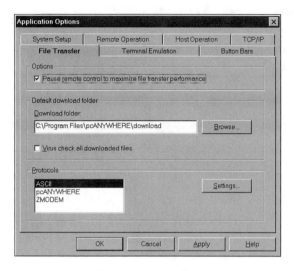

Figure 19.2   Customize the default settings for file transfers.

Table 19.2   File Transfer Options

Option	Description
Pause Remote Control to Maximize File Transfer Performance	Checked, improves speed of the transfer; unchecked, enables you to run remote control and file transfer at the same time.
Download Folder	Enter a path to the folder that will hold downloaded files.
Virus Check All Downloaded Files	Checked, examines files for viruses using Norton AntiVirus.
Protocols	Choose the protocol that is used by the online service. Choose Settings to configure the protocol.

In this lesson, you learned how to change your computer's name, set dialing properties, and customize file transfer. In the next lesson, you learn to modify button bars and create a TCP/IP host.

20

CUSTOMIZING BUTTON BARS AND OTHER APPLICATION OPTIONS

In this lesson, you learn how to customize button bars, set host operation options, and list TCP/IP hosts.

CUSTOMIZING BUTTON BARS

You can customize both the Action bar and the toolbar in pcANYWHERE by limiting the buttons on the Action bar, enabling toolbar buttons, and so on.

To customize button bars in pcANYWHERE, follow these steps:

1. Choose File, Application Options. The Application Options dialog box appears.

2. Choose the Button Bars tab, as shown in Figure 20.1.

3. In the Action bar area of the tab, check the buttons you want to display; unchecked items do not display.

4. Choose whether to make the Action buttons display with or without text; choosing Icon Only makes the buttons smaller.

5. In the Toolbar area, choose whether to show the Folder Browse and Folder History buttons. The Folder History button is actually a drop-down list in which you can type or select a path to folders you want to view and have recently viewed, as shown in Figure 20.2.

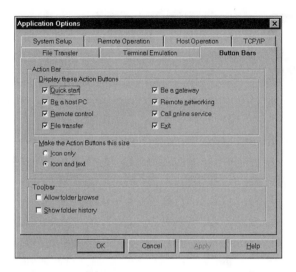

FIGURE 20.1   Customize the Action Bar and the Toolbar in pcANYWHERE.

6. Choose Apply to save the changes to the tab and leave the dialog box open to modify other settings. Or, choose OK to save the settings you've changed and close the dialog box.

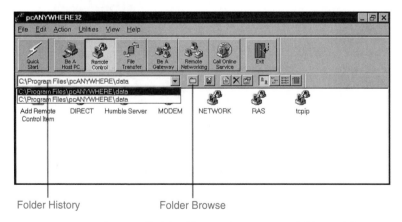

Folder History   Folder Browse

FIGURE 20.2   Use the Folder History button to quickly revisit a folder.

CREATING A TCP/IP HOST LIST

If you use TCP/IP on your network or you plan to use network connections to host PCs on your network or over the Internet, you can create a list of TCP/IP hosts that appears any time you make a network connection. You can choose the TCP/IP host from the list for a quick and easy connection shortcut.

To create a TCP/IP host list, follow these steps:

1. Choose File, Application Options. The Application Options dialog box appears.

2. Choose the TCP/IP tab, as shown in Figure 20.3.

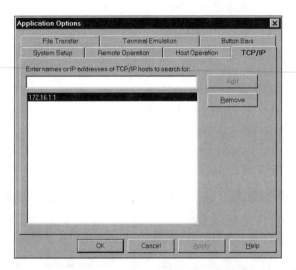

FIGURE 20.3 Create a list of hosts to choose from.

3. In the Enter names or IP addresses of TCP/IP hosts to search for text box, enter the IP address of a host. If your network uses DNS (Domain Naming System), you can enter the computer's name instead.

4. Click the Add button. Add more than one host, if you want.

5. Choose Apply to save the changes to the tab and leave the dialog box open to modify other settings. Or, choose OK to save the settings you've changed and close the dialog box.

TIP **Delete a TCP/IP Host** To delete a TCP/IP host, open the Applications Options dialog box and click the TCP/IP tab. Select the IP address or name of the host PC you want to delete and press the Remove button.

ADJUSTING TERMINAL EMULATION OPTIONS

You can customize the terminal emulators used by Windows NT and Windows 95 with pcANYWHERE. The terminal settings indicate how each type of emulation operates on your computer.

To configure terminal emulation, follow these steps:

1. Choose File, Application Options. The Application Options dialog box appears.

2. Choose the Terminal Emulation tab, as shown in Figure 20.4.

3. In the Display Options area, choose from the following options:

Automatic Font Sizing   Enables pcANYWHERE to use a font size that best suits the terminal window.

Automatic Scroll Bars   Displays horizontal and vertical scroll bars in the terminal window.

Status Line   Displays a status line that contains such information as the communications port, terminal type, and so on.

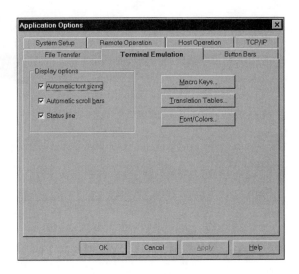

Figure 20.4 Adjust Terminal Emulation.

4. Additionally, you can click one or more of the following
buttons to further customize the Terminal Emulation
settings:

Macro Keys   Choose an existing or create a new
macro key file and configure functions for using
with the macro keys.

Fonts/Colors   Select colors and fonts to use in the
background and foreground during a connection
with an online service.

Warning Unless you're an advanced user, don't change
the translation tables in the Terminal Emulation tab of the
Applications Options dialog box.

In this lesson, you learned how to customize button bars and list
TCP/IP hosts. In the next lesson, you learn to configure a gateway
using pcANYWHERE.

Using a Gateway Connection

In this lesson, you learn how to create and modify a gateway connection, and how to start and end a gateway session.

Understanding a Gateway Connection

You use a gateway on your network to provide services to multiple users. For example, a gateway computer may supply modem connections to the users of a network. pcANYWHERE's gateway feature enables users to dial in and out so they can call computers connected to different networks.

A gateway can be either unidirectional (one-way) or bidirectional (two-way). A one-way gateway can only receive calls or send out calls; it cannot do both. A two-way gateway can receive and send calls.

Often, a two-way gateway provides its service by converting data from one communications device so a second device can receive that data. When you set up a two-way gateway service, you'll need to specify two connection devices, such as a network and modem. This enables the users of the network to send data to the gateway via the network; then the gateway converts the data to send via modem to a remote computer.

Creating a Gateway Connection

The easiest method of creating a gateway connection item is through the Wizard provided by pcANYWHERE. The Wizard creates the connection item using default settings; you can then modify those settings to suit your needs, as described later in this lesson.

 DIALIN/DIALOUT   If you want a one-way gateway, you can simply modify one of the default gateways pcANYWHERE supplies for you.

To create a gateway connection, follow these steps:

1. Click the Be A Gateway Action button. The Be A Gateway window displays (see Figure 21.1).

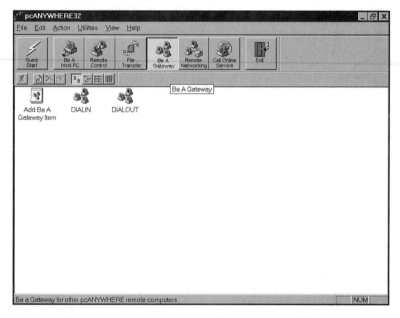

FIGURE 21.1   Choose to Be A Gateway.

2. Double-click the Add Be A Gateway Item icon to start the Wizard.

3. Enter a name for the gateway in the first Wizard dialog box. If you want the gateway to be two-way, click the check box in front of Allow Connections in Both Directions. Choose Next.

4. In the second Wizard dialog box (see Figure 21.2), choose the device(s) to use with the gateway. Click Next.

FIGURE 21.2 Enter two devices for a gateway.

5. In the last Wizard dialog box, deselect the Automatically Launch this Gateway check box and choose Finish. You'll want to configure some additional settings before launching the gateway. Choose Finish. pcANYWHERE adds the gateway icon to your Be A Gateway window.

MODIFYING A GATEWAY CONNECTION ITEM

You can modify the gateway settings, including devices, settings, and security options, at any time.

To modify a connection item's properties, follow these steps:

1. In the Be A Gateway window, right-click the gateway connection item to be modified and choose Properties from the shortcut menu.

2. The gateway's Properties dialog box appears, as shown in Figure 21.3. See the following sections for more information about changing options.

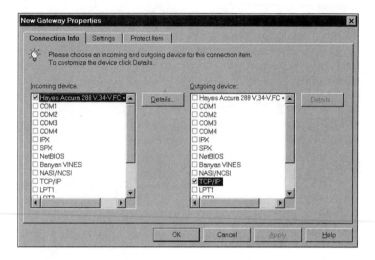

FIGURE 21.3 Modify the gateway connection item's settings.

MODIFYING CONNECTION INFO

The Connection Info tab of the Properties dialog box displays two lists of devices you can choose to use with the gateway—one for incoming and one for outgoing connections. Since the gateway receives input from one source and sends that input to another source, you must specify two devices, even if you're configuring a one-way connection item.

Choose the devices you want to use for the gateway connection item in the Connection Info tab. When you're done, choose Apply to save the changes to the tab and leave the dialog box open to modify other settings, or choose OK to save the settings you've changed and close the dialog box.

CHANGING SETTINGS

The settings in the item's Properties dialog box enable you to choose bidirectional operation, set timeout, or assign a class for the gateway.

Bidirectional Operation   Enables the gateway to send and receive communications.

Class   A name that indicates the gateway is a part of a group of gateways. Optional.

To change settings, follow these steps:

1. In the item's Properties dialog box, choose the Settings tab, as shown in Figure 21.4.

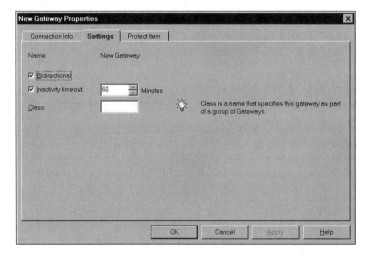

FIGURE 21.4   Settings enable you to specify direction and timeout.

2. Choose the Bidirectional check box if you'll use the gateway for two-way connections; otherwise, clear the check box.

3. If you want to specify a timeout period, click the Inactivity Timeout check box and enter a number, in minutes, for pcANYWHERE to wait before automatically disconnecting the connection.

4. Optionally, enter a name or other designation in the Class text box.

 TIP **Gateway Classifications** You might want to classify your gateway connection based on the speed of the modem; for instance, 14point4 or 28dot8 might be a classification of a group of gateways that connect using those speeds.

5. When you're done, choose Apply to save the changes to the tab and leave the dialog box open to modify other settings, or choose OK to save the settings you've changed and close the dialog box.

PROTECTING AN ITEM

As with other connection items you've created in pcANYWHERE, you can protect a gateway item from intruders to your computer. You use the Protect Item tab to set a password that sets security for the connection item. If you enter a password, only those who know the password can view or change the item's properties.

To protect the connection item, follow these steps:

1. In the Protect Item tab of the remote control connection item's Properties dialog box, enter a password in the Password text box.

2. Enter the same password in the Confirm Password text box.

3. Choose either or both of the following check boxes to apply to the password:

> Required to View Properties   Requires a password for anyone to view the item's Properties dialog box.
>
> Required to Modify Properties   Requires a password for anyone to change the options in the item's Properties dialog box.

4. Click Apply to save the changes to the tab and continue to make changes within the Properties dialog box. Alternatively, choose OK to close the dialog box and accept changes.

STARTING THE GATEWAY

pcANYWHERE loads the gateway connection item into the computer's memory and waits until an incoming or outgoing call is made. When a connection is made, the gateway computer forwards the call without the caller seeing or participating in the process.

To start a gateway, follow these steps:

1. Open the Be A Gateway window.

2. Double-click the connection item. After checking for the appropriate connection devices, the connection item appears on-screen or minimizes, depending on your configuration settings.

3. Figure 21.5 shows the pcANYWHERE Waiting dialog box for the gateway connection item.

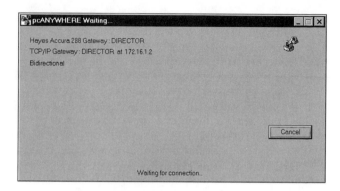

Figure 21.5   When a connection is made, the gateway converts the data and sends it to the receiving PC.

Ending the Gateway

To stop the gateway from waiting for or accepting calls, click the Cancel button in the pcANYWHERE Waiting dialog box.

In this lesson, you learned how to create and modify a gateway connection and how to start and end the gateway. In the next lesson, you learn to use pcANYWHERE's utilities.

RECORDING SESSIONS AND SAVING SCREENS

22

In this lesson, you learn to use pcANYWHERE's utilities to record sessions and save screens.

RECORDING SESSIONS

You can record the activities that occur during a session so you can later view the recording for information, troubleshooting, and so on. pcANYWHERE enables you to record the entire session, or you can record only those activities online that you need to record; in other words, you can start and stop the recording of a session at any time within the session.

TIP **Record Complex Instructions** You can use the recording utility to record complex instructions, steps, rules, or other data the user of the host PC conveys online.

To record a session while online as a remote control PC, follow these steps:

1. Choose the Control menu, pcANYWHERE, Recording. The Select Recording File dialog box appears, as shown in Figure 22.1.

2. Enter a location and file name for your file and choose Save.

FIGURE 22.1 Enter a name for the recorded file.

3. pcANYWHERE adds the Start/Stop Session Recording button to your toolbar (see Figure 22.2). Click the button at any time to pause recording; then click it again to restart recording. When you start recording again, you'll be prompted to save the new recording to a file name.

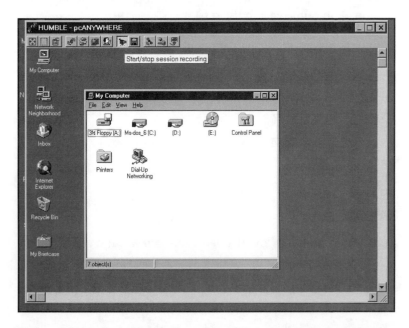

FIGURE 22.2 Record only the parts of the session you need to by pausing the recording when there's nothing happening.

4. To stop the session completely, click the Start/Stop Session Recording button.

TIP   **Record an Online Service Session**   To record an online service connection during a session, choose File, Recording and follow steps 1-4.

PLAYING A SESSION BACK

After you record a session, you can play it back within pcANYWHERE. pcANYWHERE assigns the RCD extension to recorded files. While you're replaying a session, you can also save the screen from the session as a screen shot that you can later print.

To play a session back after you've disconnected, follow these steps:

1. In pcANYWHERE, not the session window, choose Utilities, Playback Sessions/Screens.

2. The Select Playback File dialog box appears (see Figure 22.3).

FIGURE 22.3   Select the file you want to play back.

3. Select the file and choose Open. The Playback Options dialog box appears (see Figure 22.4).

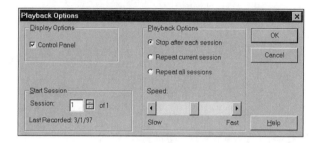

FIGURE 22.4   Choose options for playing back the session.

4. Choose options for the playback, as follows:

Control Panel   Check to display a dialog box that enables you to stop, pause, speed up, and slow down the playback.

Session   Enter the number of the session, if you've recorded multiple sessions by pausing and recording during the session.

Stop After Each Session   Stops the playback after each of multiple sessions so you can choose another. Choose the Skip to Next Session button to start the next session.

Repeat Current Session   Plays the session continuously.

Repeat All Sessions   Plays each session through continuously.

Speed   Sets the speed to play back; you can also set the speed during the playback with the Control Panel.

5. Choose OK. pcANYWHERE plays the session back and includes a Playback Control Panel for your use during the playback session. Figure 22.5 shows the Playback Control Panel. Stop a playback by clicking the Stop button on the Playback Control Panel.

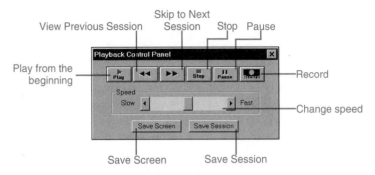

FIGURE 22.5   Use the Playback Control Panel to stop, pause, play, or record over a session.

Following is a description of the components of the Playback Control Panel:

Play   Starts the session over from the beginning.

Skip to Next Session   Jumps to the next recorded session.

View Previous Session   Jumps to the last recorded session.

Pause   Pauses and restarts the playback; click once to pause and a second time to restart.

Stop   Halts the playback.

Record   Saves the session, or appends it, to the existing file.

Save Session   Saves the session to a binary file.

Binary file   A file consisting of binary information; a base-2 numbering system using a combination of the digits 0 and 1 to represent all values.

SAVING SCREENS

You can save a screen, either during a session or from a playback of a recorded session. Saving a screen is like taking a picture of the screen with a camera. You can play back screen shots and even print them. Screens save with the SCN extension.

To save a screen during a session, follow these steps:

1. During a remote control session, choose the Control menu, pcANYWHERE, Save Screen. During an online service session, choose File, Save Screen. The Select Save Screen File dialog box appears (see Figure 22.6).

Figure 22.6   Save as many screens as it takes to record a session.

2. Enter the file name, choose the location, and click Open to save the screen.

> **TIP** **Screen Shot** To save a screen of a session playback, click the Pause button in the Playback Control Panel and then click the Save Screen button. The Select Save Screen File dialog box appears in which you name the file and choose a location. Choose Open to save the shot.

PLAYING BACK A SCREEN

You can play back one or several screen shots after the session is ended. You use the Utilities menu in the pcANYWHERE window, as follows:

1. To display the screen shot, choose Utilities, Playback Sessions/Screens. The Select Playback File dialog box appears.

2. Choose Files of Type, Screen Files (SCN).

3. Choose the folder, if necessary, and then select the screen shot and choose Open. pcANYWHERE opens the screen shot to your screen (see Figure 22.7).

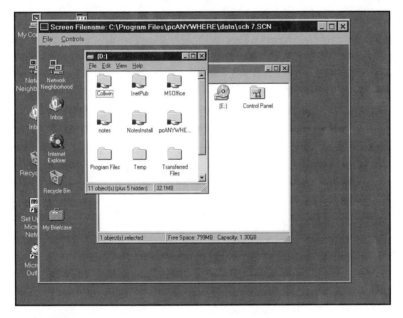

FIGURE 22.7 Display screen shots of your sessions.

4. To close a screen shot, click the Close button.

In this lesson, you learned to use pcANYWHERE's utilities to record sessions and save screens. In the next lesson, you learn to log sessions.

LESSON 23

LOGGING SESSIONS AND VIEWING REPORTS

In this lesson, you learn to log sessions and create and view log reports.

LOGGING SESSIONS

You can record statistics and information about a session to track, for example, who has made connections to a host PC, when the session started and ended, and so on. A remote user, on the other hand, can track which hosts were called and file transfers that took place during the sessions.

To create a log file of a session in the remote control PC, follow these steps:

1. Open the Remote Control window by clicking the appropriate button on the Action bar.

2. Right-click the connection item and choose Properties. The item's Properties dialog box appears.

3. Click the Automated Tasks tab and choose Save Session Statistics in Log File.

4. Choose OK.

To create a log file of a session in a remote PC for an Online session, follow these steps:

1. Open the Online Service window and right-click the connection item.

2. Choose Properties from the shortcut menu.

3. Choose the Session tab.

4. Check the Save Session Statistics in Activity Log File option.

5. Choose OK to close the dialog box.

To create a log file on a host PC, follow these steps:

1. Open the Be A Host PC window.

2. Right-click the connection item and choose Properties from the shortcut menu. The Properties dialog box appears.

3. Choose the Callers tab.

4. Choose Specify Individual Caller Privileges.

5. Right-click a caller and choose Properties from the shortcut menu.

6. Choose the Advanced tab and choose the Save Session Statistics in Activity Log option.

7. Choose OK.

CREATING AND VIEWING A LOG REPORT

When you disconnect from a session for which you've specified a log be created, pcANYWHERE prompts you for a Log Comment, as shown in Figure 23.1. After disconnecting from a session, you can create and view a report on the activity.

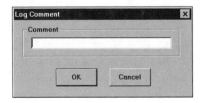

FIGURE 23.1 Enter a comment describing the session.

To create and view a log report, follow these steps:

1. In pcANYWHERE, choose Utilities, Activity Log Processing. The Activity Log Processing dialog box appears, as shown in Figure 23.2.

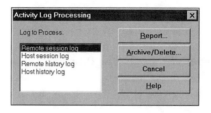

FIGURE 23.2   Create a report of the logged information.

2. Choose the log you want to process; for example, choose Remote Session Log if you want to create a report of the remote control session you just had.

3. Click Report. The Select Destination File for Output dialog box appears. Choose a location and enter a name for the log.

4. Click the Open button; the Host and Remote Session Log Report dialog box appears, as shown in Figure 23.3.

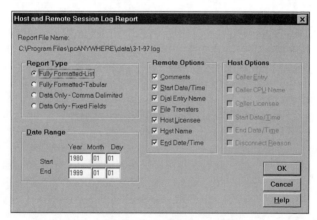

FIGURE 23.3   Select the options for the log report.

5. Enter a date in the Date Range; notice the default date is 1980 to 1999.

6. Generally, choose a Fully Formatted List for the Report Type; it's the easiest to decipher. Select any options you want to apply to your report.

7. Choose OK. pcANYWHERE displays a dialog box that tells you the path and file name of the report and asks if you want to view it now.

8. Choose Yes to view the report; choose No to view it later. Figure 23.4 shows a report log of a remote control session.

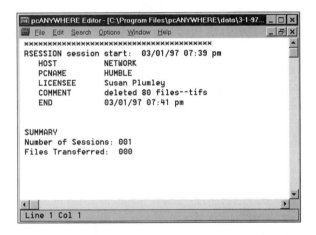

FIGURE **23.4**   View statistics of the session in a report log.

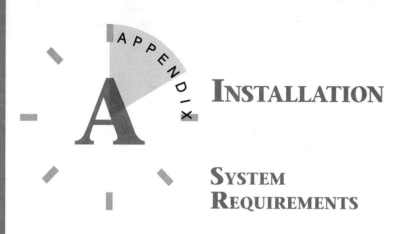

INSTALLATION

SYSTEM REQUIREMENTS

Following is a list of the recommended hardware and software you'll need to install and use pcANYWHERE32 version 7.5. By using the recommended system requirements as opposed to the minimum requirements, the program runs more efficiently and effectively.

Hardware:

486, Pentium, or higher microprocessor

8M RAM or more

16M free disk space, more to store downloaded files

Windows 95 or Windows NT 3.51 or later (server or workstation)

INSTALLING TO A STANDALONE

You install pcANYWHERE to a standalone computer, one not attached to a network, and use the program with a modem or dial-up connection.

To install pcANYWHERE to a standalone computer, follow these steps:

1. Turn on the computer. Insert the first disk into the computer's floppy disk drive.

2. Choose Start, Run.

3. In the Run dialog box, enter **a:\setup.exe** and press
   Enter. pcANYWHERE installs the files to your computer
   with the use of an installation wizard. Change disks when
   prompted.

4. When prompted, enter your name and company's name.
   Click the Next button.

5. When prompted, supply the drive and folder name to
   which you want to install the program; you can accept
   the default drive and folder, if you want. Click the Next
   button.

6. Follow the directions in the wizard dialog boxes. When
   installation is complete, the wizard dialog boxes displayed
   enable you to register the product by modem. You can
   accept this default or click the Skip button to complete
   the installation process.

7. In the last wizard dialog box, click the Finish button.

INSTALLING TO A NETWORK SERVER

You install pcANYWHERE to a network server (NT Server 3.51 or
4.0) to enable use of pcANYWHERE over the network. After installing the program to a server, workstations connected to the
network can install the program to their computers from the network instead of from diskette. Installation is much quicker and
configuration for network use is automatic when a user installs
the program from the server.

Installing to the server takes three distinct steps:

1. Installing the installation files to the server.

2. Installing the workstation files to the server.

3. Configuring the program for network use.

INSTALLING THE FILES

To install pcANYWHERE to your network server, follow these steps:

1. Start NT and log in as the Administrator.

2. Insert the first installation disk into the disk drive and choose Start, Run.

3. In the Run dialog box, type **a:\setup /a** and choose OK. pcANYWHERE installs the necessary files. Insert the program diskettes when prompted.

4. When prompted, enter your name and the company name. Click Next.

5. When prompted, specify the folder in which to install the program or accept the default. Click Next.

6. Follow the directions in the wizard dialog boxes. Register the copy of pcANYWHERE, if you want, or skip the process for now.

7. In the Explorer, select the folder to which pcANYWHERE is installed and share it.

Next, you need to install pcANYWHERE on the server as a workstation installation before you can configure the program for administration. To install pcANYWHERE on the server as a workstation, follow the steps outlined in "Installing to a Network Workstation," and then refer back to the following section.

CONFIGURING THE PROGRAM FOR USE ON THE NETWORK

After you install the program to the Windows NT server, both as a server and a workstation (see next section), you can configure the application for network use.

To configure pcANYWHERE for network administration, follow these steps:

1. On the server, choose Start, Run. Enter the network pathname followed by the application for configuration: **winaw32.exe /a**.

2. Choose OK. When prompted, enter a password to be used for administering the program. Confirm the password.

3. Choose Administrator, Shared Data. The Shared Data dialog box appears.

4. In the Remote Control tab, check to make sure the following things are correct:

   • The Allow Folder Change check box is checked, or selected.

   • The path and folder name in the Use Folder text box is correct; you can either accept the default folder or enter another folder, if you prefer.

5. Repeat step 4 with the Online Service, Be a Host PC, and Gateway tabs.

6. Choose the Computer Name Selection tab and choose one of the following options:

   • Allow User Defined   Enables the user to provide the PC's name.

   • Windows Computer Name Only   Directs pcANYWHERE to automatically use the workstation's computer name provided in the Windows installation.

7. Choose OK to close the Shared Data dialog box. Click the Close button to exit the pcANYWHERE administration program.

INSTALLING TO A NETWORK WORKSTATION

Use the following directions to install the program to any workstation connected to the server on a network. The workstation can be running Windows 95, Windows NT 3.51 or 4.0 Workstation, or Windows NT 3.51 or 4.0 Server.

To install pcANYWHERE to a workstation, follow these steps:

1. Choose Start, Run. The Run dialog box appears.

2. In the Open text box, enter the network path and **setup\setup.exe** and choose OK. For example, you might enter **\\program files\pcanywhere\ setup\setup.exe**.

3. Follow the directions on-screen to enter the user's name and company name. Click Next.

4. When prompted, enter a new path and folder to which to store the program files or accept the default. Click Next.

5. When the installation is complete, you'll be prompted to restart Windows.

RUNNING pcANYWHERE FOR THE FIRST TIME

The first time you run pcANYWHERE, you need to configure the program for network or modem use. To complete this process, follow these steps:

1. Choose Start, Programs, pcANYWHERE32 folder, and pcANYWHERE.

2. The pcANYWHERE Smart Setup Wizard dialog box appears.

3. Choose the modem to which your computer is connected, if applicable. pcANYWHERE detects your modem and automatically adds it. If you have no modem, you'll see the network device wizard dialog box.

4. In the network device wizard dialog box, choose the protocol your computer uses to attach to the network. If you're unsure, see your network administrator. Click the Next button.

5. If you plan to use a direct cable connection, select the port to which the cable will be attached. Click the Finish button.

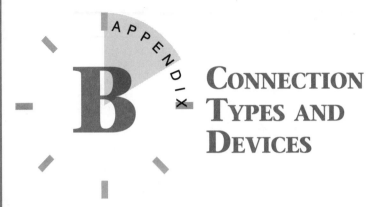

CONNECTION TYPES AND DEVICES

TYPES OF CONNECTIONS

You can connect two computers through a telephone line, network, or a combination of the two, or you can directly connect two computers using a cable between the two. Following is a list of the types of connections you can make with pcANYWHERE:

- **Modem connection** Using a modem, you can transmit data over standard telephone lines to another computer with a modem. This connection type works well when the two computers are not in proximity to each other. Also called a serial connection.

- **Direct connection** You can directly connect two computers that are side-by-side using a cable. You can either connect the two computers with a serial (null modem) cable or a parallel cable. Using a parallel cable is faster for transferring files than using a serial cable. Using a cable eliminates the need for a modem but the two computers must be close enough to physically attach the cable.

- **Network connection** You can connect two computers over a local area network (LAN), such as Novell NetWare or NT Server using a variety of protocols: NetBIOS, TCP/IP, IPX/SPX, and so on.

- **Gateway connection** You use a gateway connection between two pcANYWHERE connection types, such as a modem and network adapter card. The gateway directs outgoing messages to the next available modem and directs incoming messages to the appropriate network computer.

TYPES OF CONNECTION DEVICES

You can use a variety of connection devices to connect a computer running pcANYWHERE to another computer. Following is a list and description of the possible connection devices.

 Connection Device   A modem, network interface card, or other hardware component that enables your PC to connect to another PC enabling communications between the two.

NETWORK DEVICES

Network devices are also called protocols. Depending on the type of network your workstation connects to, you use the protocol that is appropriate. Following are the protocols you can use with pcANYWHERE:

- **IPX (Internet Packet Exchange)**   A protocol used on Novell NetWare networks to transfer data between the server and the workstations on the network.

- **SPX (Sequenced Packet Exchange)**   A set of Novell NetWare protocols that work on top of IPX to provide additional capabilities to IPX.

- **NetBIOS (Network Basic Input/Output System)** A network protocol used to manage data and network access. Often used with Windows NT, Windows for Workgroups, and Windows 95 computers.

- **Banyan VINES (Virtual Networking Software)** made by Banyan Systems   A network operating system based on a special version of the UNIX System V. Vines provides all server functions, including those of a communications/modem server.

- **NASI/NCSI (NetWare Asynchronous Services Interface/NetWare Asynchronous Communications Services)**   A device driver for a NetWare network.

- **TCP/IP (Transmission Control Protocol/Internet Protocol)**   A set of communications protocols supported by a large number of hardware and software vendors, including Microsoft networks, Novell NetWare networks, and pcANYWHERE.

CABLE DEVICES

You can use a cable to connect two computers in close proximity so that communications with pcANYWHERE is possible. These computers can transfer files, remotely control one another, and otherwise take advantage of other pcANYWHERE features.

Port   A port is a hardware device that enables you to connect various peripheral devices, such as a modem or printer, to your computer.

Following is a list of cable device hardware you can use with pcANYWHERE. The differences between the ports has to do with how data is transferred. You need one type of cable (null modem or serial cable) to use the serial port for communications and a different type of cable (parallel cable) to use the parallel port.

- **Serial Ports** transmit data from computer to computer, one bit at a time. Sending and receiving devices must be configured using the same communications parameters, such as baud rate and parity. The serial ports on a computer are: COM1, COM2, COM3, and COM4.

- **Parallel Ports** transmit data from computer to computer, so that all bits are transmitted at the same time. A parallel port manages data at 8 bits at a time. Parallel ports include LPT1 and LPT2.

MODEM

A modem (contraction of MODulator/DEModulator) is a device that enables your computer to transmit information over a telephone line. The modem translates between the digital signals that the computer uses and the analog signals suitable for transmission over telephone lines.

Your modem is identified to pcANYWHERE by its manufacturer's name and model.

INDEX

W-Z

Check out Que® Books on the World Wide Web
http://quecorp.com

As the biggest software release in computer history, Windows 95 continues to redefine the computer industry. Click here for the latest info on our Windows 95 books

Make computing quick and easy with these products designed exclusively for new and casual users

Examine the latest releases in word processing, spreadsheets, operating systems, and suites

The Internet, The World Wide Web, CompuServe®, America Online®, Prodigy® —it's a world of ever-changing information. Don't get left behind!

Find out about new additions to our site, new bestsellers and hot topics

In-depth information on high-end topics: find the best reference books for databases, programming, networking, and client/server technologies

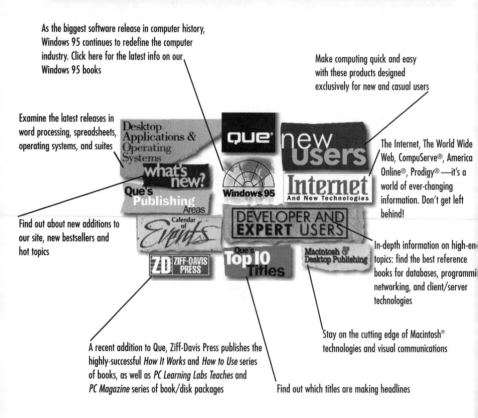

A recent addition to Que, Ziff-Davis Press publishes the highly-successful *How It Works* and *How to Use* series of books, as well as *PC Learning Labs Teaches* and *PC Magazine* series of book/disk packages

Stay on the cutting edge of Macintosh® technologies and visual communications

Find out which titles are making headlines

With 6 separate publishing groups, Que develops products for many specific market segments and areas of computer technology. Explore our Web Site and you'll find information on best-selling titles, newly published titles, upcoming products, authors, and much more.

- Stay informed on the latest industry trends and products available
- Visit our online bookstore for the latest information and editions
- Download software from Que's library of the best shareware and freeware

Complete and Return this Card
for a *FREE* Computer Book Catalog

Thank you for purchasing this book! You have purchased a
superior computer book written expressly for your needs. To
continue to provide the kind of up-to-date, pertinent coverage
you've come to expect from us, we need to hear from you.
Please take a minute to complete and return this self-addressed,
postage-paid form. In return, we'll send you a free catalog of all
our computer books on topics ranging from word processing to
programming and the internet.

Mr. ☐   Mrs. ☐   Ms. ☐   Dr. ☐

Name (first) ☐☐☐☐☐☐☐☐☐ (M.I.) ☐ (last) ☐☐☐☐☐☐☐☐☐☐☐☐☐

Address ☐☐☐☐☐☐☐☐☐☐☐☐☐☐☐☐☐☐☐☐☐☐☐☐☐☐☐

☐☐☐☐☐☐☐☐☐☐☐☐☐☐☐☐☐☐☐☐☐☐☐☐☐☐☐

City ☐☐☐☐☐☐☐☐☐☐☐ State ☐☐ Zip ☐☐☐☐☐ ☐☐☐☐

Phone ☐☐☐ ☐☐☐ ☐☐☐☐ Fax ☐☐☐ ☐☐☐ ☐☐☐☐

Company Name ☐☐☐☐☐☐☐☐☐☐☐☐☐☐☐☐☐☐☐☐☐☐☐

E-mail address ☐☐☐☐☐☐☐☐☐☐☐☐☐☐☐☐☐☐☐☐☐☐☐☐

1. Please check at least (3) influencing factors for purchasing this book.

Front or back cover information on book .... ☐
Special approach to the content .... ☐
Completeness of content .... ☐
Author's reputation .... ☐
Publisher's reputation .... ☐
Book cover design or layout .... ☐
Index or table of contents of book .... ☐
Price of book .... ☐
Special effects, graphics, illustrations .... ☐
Other (Please specify): _____ ☐

2. How did you first learn about this book?

Internet Site .... ☐
Saw in Macmillan Computer
　Publishing catalog .... ☐
Recommended by store personnel .... ☐
Saw the book on bookshelf at store .... ☐
Recommended by a friend .... ☐
Received advertisement in the mail .... ☐
Saw an advertisement in: _____ ☐
Read book review in: _____ ☐
Other (Please specify): _____ ☐

3. How many computer books have you purchased in the last six months?

This book only .... ☐　3 to 5 books .... ☐
2 books .... ☐　More than 5 .... ☐

4. Where did you purchase this book?

Bookstore .... ☐
Computer Store .... ☐
Consumer Electronics Store .... ☐
Department Store .... ☐
Office Club .... ☐
Warehouse Club .... ☐
Mail Order .... ☐
Direct from Publisher .... ☐
Internet site .... ☐
Other (Please specify): .... ☐

5. How long have you been using a computer?

Less than 6 months .. ☐　6 months to a year ..... ☐
1 to 3 years .... ☐　More than 3 years ...... ☐

6. What is your level of experience with personal computers and with the subject of this book?

	With PC's	With subject of book
New	☐	☐
Casual	☐	☐
Accomplished	☐	☐
Expert	☐	☐

Source Code — ISBN: 0-7897-1269-5

7. Which of the following best describes your job title?

Administrative Assistant .... ☐
Coordinator .... ☐
Manager/Supervisor .... ☐
Director .... ☐
Vice President .... ☐
President/CEO/COO .... ☐
Lawyer/Doctor/Medical Professional .... ☐
Teacher/Educator/Trainer .... ☐
Engineer/Technician .... ☐
Consultant .... ☐
Not employed/Student/Retired .... ☐
Other (Please specify): .... ☐

8. Which of the following best describes the area of the company your job title falls under?

Accounting .... ☐
Engineering .... ☐
Manufacturing .... ☐
Marketing .... ☐
Operations .... ☐
Sales .... ☐
Other (Please specify): .... ☐

9. What is your age?

Under 20 .... ☐
21-29 .... ☐
30-39 .... ☐
40-49 .... ☐
50-59 .... ☐
60-over .... ☐

10. Are you:

Male .... ☐
Female .... ☐

11. Which computer publications do you read regularly? (Please list)

_____
_____
_____
_____
_____
_____
_____
_____
_____
_____

Comments: _____

Fold here and scotch-tape to n

||'''|'|'''|''|'''||'|'|'|'|''|||'|'|''||'|''|

MACMILLAN COMPUTER PUBLISHING USA

A VIACOM COMPANY

Technical ---- Support:

If you need assistance with the information in this book or with a CD/Disk
accompanying the book, please access the Knowledge Base on our Web
site at **http://www.superlibrary.com/general/support**. Our most
Frequently Asked Questions are answered there. If you do not find the
answer to your questions on our Web site, you may contact Macmillan
Technical Support **(317) 581-3833** or e-mail us at **support@mcp.com**.